Mahatma Gandhi

Mahatma Gandhi

THE MAN WHO BECAME ONE WITH THE UNIVERSAL BEING

Romain Rolland

GENERAL PRESS

Published by

GENERAL PRESS

4805/24, Fourth Floor, Krishna House
Ansari Road, Daryaganj, New Delhi - 110002
Ph : 011-23282971, 45795759
E-mail : generalpressindia@gmail.com

www.generalpress.in

First Edition : 2022

ISBN : 9789354994722

Published by Azeem Ahmad Khan for General Press

Contents

Mohandas Karamchand Gandhi

In connection with the present essay I wish to tender my affectionate thanks to my faithful collaborator, my sister, and to my friend, Kalidas Nag, whose deep knowledge and indefatigable kindness have guided my steps through the forest of Indian thought.

I also wish to thank the publisher, S. Ganesan of Madras, for having placed, spontaneously, his publications at my disposal.

* * *

The literal translation of Mahatma, the name which the people of India gave to Gandhi, is "the great Soul," *maha*, great; *atma*, soul. The word goes back to the Upanishads, where it is used in speaking of the Supreme Being, and, through communion of Knowledge and Love, of those who become One with Him:

"He is the One Luminous, Creator of All,
Mahatma,
Always in the hearts of the people enshrined.
Revealed through Love, Intuition, and Thought,
Whoever knows Him, Immortal becomes..."

Tagore, on a visit to Ashram, Gandhi's favorite retreat, quoted this stanza, referring to the Apostle.

PART ONE

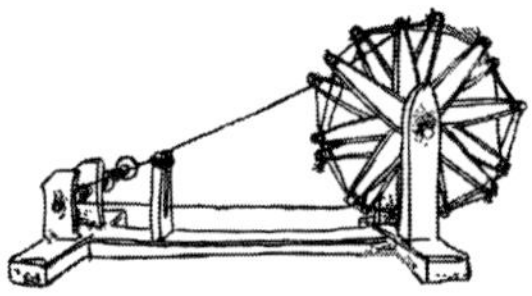

CHAPTER 1

Dark, tranquil eyes. A small frail man, a thin face with large protruding ears. His head covered with a little white cap, his body clothed in coarse white cloth, barefooted. He lives on rice and fruit and drinks only water. He sleeps on the floor—sleeps very little, and works incessantly. His body does not seem to count at all. There is nothing striking about him, at first, except his expression of "great patience and great love." W. W. Pearson, who met him in South Africa in 1918, instinctively thought of St. Francis of Assisi. There is an almost childlike simplicity about him.[1] His manner is gentle and courteous even when dealing with adversaries,[2] and he is of immaculate sincerity.[3] He is modest and unassuming, to the point of sometimes seeming almost timid, hesitant, in making an assertion. Yet you feel his indomitable spirit. He makes no compromises and never tries to hide a mistake. Nor is he afraid to admit having been in the wrong. Diplomacy is unknown to him; he shuns oratorical effect or, rather, never thinks about it;

1. As C. F. Andrews says, "He laughs like a child and adores children."
2. "Few can resist the charm of his personality. His bitterest enemies become courteous when confronted with his beautiful courtesy." (Joseph J. Doke.)
3. "Every departure from truth, no matter how trifling, is intolerable to him." (C. F. Andrews.)

and he shrinks unconsciously from the great popular demonstrations organized in his honor. Literally "ill with the multitude that adores him,"[1] he distrusts majorities and fears "mobocracy" and the unbridled passions of the populace. He feels at ease only in a minority, and is happiest when, in meditative solitude, he can listen to the "still small voice" within.[2]

This is the man who has stirred three hundred million people to revolt, who has shaken the foundations of the British Empire, and who has introduced into human politics the strongest religious impetus of the last two thousand years.

1. "He is not a passionate orator; his manner is calm and serene and he appeals particularly to the intelligence. But his serenity places the subject he discusses in the clearest light. The inflexions of his voice are not varied but they are intensely sincere. He never makes any gestures with his arms, in fact he rarely even moves a finger. But his luminous words, expressed in terse, concise sentences, carry conviction. He never abandons a subject before he feels that he has made it perfectly clear." (Joseph J. Doke.)
2. "Young India," March 2, 1922. The dates cited in the motes of this volume refer to the date of publication of Gandhi's articles in "Young India."

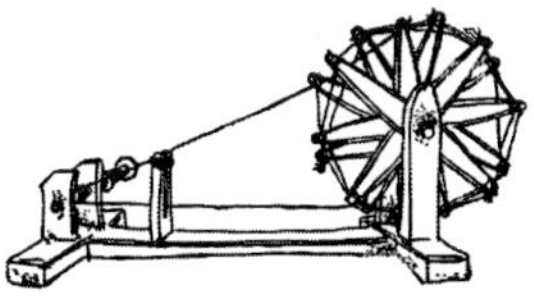

CHAPTER 2

His real name is Mohandas Karamchand Gandhi. He was born in a little semi-independent state in the northwestern part of India, at Porbandar, the "White City" on the sea of Oman, October 2, 1868. He comes of an ardent and active race, which to this day has been split by civil strife; a practical race, commercially keen, which established trade relations all the way from Aden to Zanzibar. Gandhi's father and grandfather were both leaders of the people and met with persecution because of their independent spirit. Both were forced to flee for safety, their lives in peril. Gandhi's family was well-to-do and belonged to a cultivated class of society, but it was not of superior caste. His parents were followers of the Jaïn school of Hinduism, which regards *ahimsa*,[1] the doctrine of non-injury to any form of life, as one of its basic principles. This was the doctrine which Gandhi was to proclaim victoriously throughout the world. The Jaïnists believe that the principle of love, not intelligence, is the road

1. *A*, privative, *himsa*, to do evil. Hence, *ahimsa*, principle of not harming any form of life, nonviolence. It is one of Hinduism's most ancient precepts, proclaimed by Mahavira, the founder of Jaïnism, by Buddha, as well as by the disciples of Vishnu.

which leads to God. The Mahatma's father cared little for wealth and material values, and left scarcely any to his family, having given almost everything away to charity. Gandhi's mother was a very devout woman, a sort of Hindu St. Elisabeth, fasting, giving alms to the poor, and nursing the sick. In Gandhi's family the Ramayana was read regularly. His first teacher was a Brahman who taught him to memorize the texts of Vishnu.[1] In later years Gandhi expressed regret at not being a better Sanskrit scholar, and one of his grievances against English education in India is that it makes the natives lose the treasures of their own language. Gandhi became, however, a profound student of Hindu scriptures, although he read the Vedas and the Upanishads in translation only.[2]

While still a boy he passed through a severe religious crisis. Shocked at the idolatrous form sometimes assumed by Hinduism, he became, or imagined he became, an atheist, and to prove that religion meant nothing to him he and some friends went so far as to eat meat, a frightful sacrilege for a Hindu. And Gandhi nearly perished with disgust and mortification.[3] He was engaged at the age of eight and married at the age of twelve.[4] At nineteen

---

1. He attended the elementary school of Porbandar till the age of seven and then the public school of Rajkot till ten. After that he went to the high school of Katyavar until, at the age of seventeen, he entered the University of Ahmedabad.
2. He described his childhood in a speech at the Pariah Conference, April 13, 1921.
3. Long afterward he told Joseph Doke of the anguish he had suffered after eating meat. He was unable to sleep; he felt like a murderer.
4. He is not in favor of child marriages, however, and made a campaign against them, on the ground that they weaken the race. In exceptional cases, however, he says that such unions, sealed before the individual's character is molded, may build up between husband and wife an exceptionally beautiful relationship of sympathy and harmony. Gandhi's own wife is an admirable example of

he was sent to England to complete his studies at the University of London and at the law school. Before his leaving India, his mother made him take the three vows of Jaïn, which prescribe abstention from wine, meat, and sexual intercourse.

He arrived in London in September, 1888, and after the first few months of uncertainty and deception, during which, as he says, he "wasted a lot of time and money trying to become an Englishman," he buckled down to hard work and led a strictly regulated life. Some friends gave him a copy of the Bible, but the time to understand it had not yet come. But it was during his stay in London that he realized for the first time the beauty of the Bhagavad Gitâ. He was carried away by it. It was the light the exiled Hindu had been seeking, and it gave him back his faith. He realized that for him salvation could lie only in Hinduism.[1]

He returned to India in 1891, a rather sad home-coming, for his mother had just died, and the news of her death had been withheld from him. Soon afterward he began practicing law at the Supreme Court of Bombay. He abandoned this career a few years later, having come to look upon it as immoral. But even while practicing law he used to make a point of reserving the right to abandon a case if he had reason to believe it unjust.

At this stage of his career he met various people who stirred in him a presentiment as to his future mission in life. He was influenced by two men in particular. One of them was the "Uncrowned King of Bombay," the Parsi Dadabhai, and the other Professor Gokhale. Gokhale was one of the leading statesmen in India and one of the first to introduce educational reforms, while Dadabhai, according to Gandhi, was the real founder of the Indian

---

this. Mrs. Gandhi shared all her husband's trials and adversities with unfailing steadfastness of purpose and indomitable courage.

1. Speech of April 13, 1921.

nationalist movement. Both men combined the highest wisdom and learning with the utmost simplicity and gentleness.[1] It was Dadabhai who, in trying to moderate Gandhi's youthful ardor, gave him, in 1892, his first real lesson in *ahimsa* by teaching him to apply heroic passivity—if two such words may be linked—to public life by fighting evil, not by evil, but by love. A little later we will discuss this magic word of *ahimsa*, the sublime message of India to the world.

1. These two men, precursors, have suffered from the ingratitude and forgetfulness of younger generations. Their political ideal having been surpassed, their efforts in paving the way have been deprecated. Gandhi, however, always realized their contribution to the cause and remained true to them, particularly to Gokhale, for whom he felt a deep and almost religious affection. He frequently speaks of Gokhale and Dadabhai as men whom Young India should venerate. (See "Hind Swaraj, Letter to the Parsecs, Young India," March 23, 1921, and the Confession of Faith, July 13, 1921.)

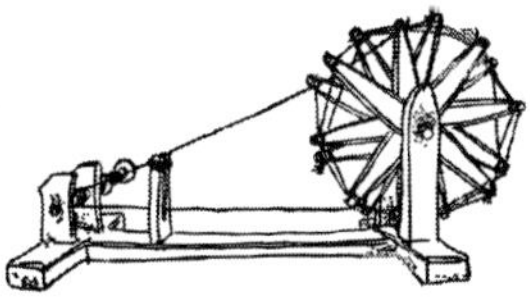

CHAPTER 3

Gandhi's activity may be divided into two periods. From 1898 to 1914 its field was South Africa; from 1914 to 1922, India.

That Gandhi could carry on the South-African campaign for more than twenty years without awakening any special comment in Europe is a proof of the incredible short-sightedness of our political leaders, historians, thinkers, and believers, for Gandhi's efforts constituted a soul's epopee, unequaled in our times, not only because of the intensity and the constancy of the sacrifice required, but because of the final triumph.

In 1890-91 some 150,000 Indian emigrants were settled in South Africa, most of them having taken up abode in Natal. The white population resented their presence, and the Government encouraged the xenophobia of the whites by a series of oppressive measures designed to prevent the immigration of Asiatics and to oblige those already settled in Africa to leave. Through systematic persecution the life of the Indians in Africa was made intolerable; they were burdened with overwhelming taxes and subjected to the most humiliating police ordinances and outrages of all sorts, ranging from the looting and destruction of shops and property to lynching, all under cover of "white" civilization.

In 1893 Gandhi was called to Pretoria on an important case. He was not familiar with the situation in South Africa, but from the very first he met with illuminating experiences. Gandhi, a Hindu of high race, who had always been received with the greatest courtesy in England and Europe, and who until then had looked upon the whites as his natural friends, suddenly found himself the butt of the vilest affronts. In Natal, and particularly in Dutch Transvaal, he was thrown out of hotels and trains, insulted, beaten, and kicked. He would have returned to India at once if he had not been bound by contract to remain a year in South Africa. During these twelve months he learned the art of self-control, but all the time he longed for his contract to expire, so that he might return to India. But when at last he was about to leave, he learned that the South-African Government was planning to pass a bill depriving the Indians of the franchise. The Indians in Africa were helpless, unable to defend themselves; they were completely unorganized and demoralized. They had no leader, no one to guide them. Gandhi felt that it was his duty to defend them. He realized it would be wrong to leave. The cause of the disinherited Indians became his. He gave himself up to it, and remained in Africa.

Then began an epic struggle between spirit on one side and governmental power and brute force on the other. Gandhi was a lawyer at the time, and his first step was to prove the illegality of the Asiatic Exclusion Act from the point of view of law, and he won his case despite the most virulent opposition. In this connection he had huge petitions signed; he organized the Indian Congress at Natal, and formed an association for Indian education. A little later he founded a paper, "Indian Opinion," published in English and three Indian languages. Finally, in order to work more efficaciously for his compatriots in Africa, he decided to become one of them. He had a lucrative clientele in Johannesburg (Gokhale says Gandhi was making at that time about five or six thousand pounds a year). He gave it up to espouse poverty, like St. Francis. He abandoned all ties in order to live the life of the persecuted Indians, to share their trials. And he ennobled them thereby, for he taught them the doctrine of non-resistance. In 1904 he founded at Phoenix, near Durban, an agricultural colony along Tolstoian lines.[1] He called upon his compatriots, gave them land, and made them take the solemn oath of poverty. He took upon himself the humblest tasks.

For years the silent colony resisted the Government. It withdrew from the cities, gradually paralyzing the industrial life of the country, carrying on a sort of religious strike against which violence—all violence—was powerless, just as the violence of imperial Rome was powerless against the faith of the first Christians. Yet very few of these early Christians would have carried the doctrine of love and forgiveness so far as to help their persecutors when in danger, as Gandhi did. Whenever the South-African state was in serious difficulties Gandhi suspended the non-participation of the Indian population in public services and offered his assistance. In 1899, during the Boer War, he organized an Indian Red Cross, which was twice cited for bravery under fire.

---

1. A long letter from Tolstoi to Gandhi is published in the "Golden Number" of "Indian Opinion." It was written September 7, 1910, shortly before Tolstoi's death. Tolstoi had read "Indian Opinion," and he was gratified to hear of the Indian non-resisters. He praised their campaign and says that non-resistance is the law of love, an aspiration to form part of the communion of human souls. It is the law of Christ and of all the spiritual leaders of the world.

   My friend Paul Biroukoff found several other letters from Tolstoi to Gandhi in the Tolstoi archives at Moscow. He is planning to publish them in a volume entitled "Tolstoi and the Orient," adding them to several other letters written by Tolstoi to various great men of the East.

When the plague broke out in Johannesburg in 1904, Gandhi organized a hospital. In 1908 the natives in Natal revolted. Gandhi organized and served at the head of a corps of *brancardiers*, and the Government of Natal tendered him public thanks.

But these disinterested services did not disarm the hatred of the whites. Gandhi was frequently arrested and imprisoned,[1] and shortly after official thanks had been proffered for his services during the war he was sentenced to imprisonment and hard labor, after being beaten by the mob and left behind as dead.[2] But no abuse, no persecution, could make Gandhi renounce his ideal. On the contrary, his faith in it grew stronger for his trials. His only reply to the violence meted out to him in South Africa was the famous little book, "Hind Swaraj,"[3] published in 1908. This pamphlet on Indian home rule is the gospel of heroic love.

For twenty years the struggle lasted, reaching its bitterest phase from 1907 to 1914. Although the most intelligent and broad-minded Englishmen in Africa were opposed to it, in 1906 the South-African Government hastily passed a new Asiatic law. This led Gandhi to organize non-resistance on a large scale.

In September, 1906, a huge demonstration took place at Johannesburg, and the assembled Indians solemnly took the oath of passive resistance. The Chinese in Africa joined the Hindus; and Asiatics of all races, religions, and castes, rich and poor alike,

---

1. Gandhi himself tells in his quiet humorous way of his experiences in prison in a curious article printed in the volume, "Speeches and Writings of M. K. Gandhi," Natesan, Madras, pp. 152-178.
2. In 1907 Gandhi was the victim of the violence of his own compatriots, for his moderation was eyed with suspicion by certain Indians, while, the Government, on the other hand, did all in its power to compromise him. Gandhi, therefore, suffered from the violence of the oppressed as well as of the oppressors.
3. I will dwell on "Hind Swaraj" a little more at length, later on.

brought the same enthusiasm and abnegation to the cause. The Asiatics were thrown into prison by the thousand, and as the jails were not large enough, they were hurled into the mine-pits. But it was as if the prisons fascinated these people whom General Smuts, their persecutor, called "conscientious objectors." Three times Gandhi was thrown into jail,[1] while others died as martyrs. The movement grew. In 1918 it spread from the Transvaal to Natal. Huge strikes and monster meetings, masses of Hindus marching across Transvaal, alarmed and excited public opinion in Africa and Asia. All India was stirred to indignation, and the viceroy, Lord Hardinge, driven by public opinion, finally lodged a protest against the Government of South Africa.

The indomitable tenacity and the magic of the "Great Soul" operated and won out: force had to bow down before heroic gentleness.[2] The man most bitterly opposed to the Indians, General Smuts, who in 1909 had said he would never erase from the statutes a measure prejudicial to the Indians, confessed, five years later, in 1914, that he was glad to do away with it.[3] An imperial commission backed Gandhi up on almost every point. In 1914 an act abolished the three-pound poll-tax, while Natal was opened to all Indians desirous of settling there as free workers. After twenty years of sacrifice non-resistance was triumphant.

---

1. Joseph J. Doke, interesting because of his interviews with Gandhi, tells in the last chapter of his book how, in 1908, Gandhi was led to the fort of Johannesburg in prison garb and thrown into a cell with Chinese common-law criminals of the worst sort.
2. Two high-minded Englishmen, C. F. Andrews and W. W. Pearson, seconded Gandhi's efforts by all means within their power.
3. Gandhi refers to this in an article dated May 12, 1920.

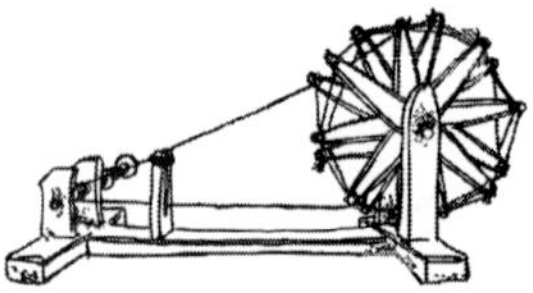

CHAPTER 4

When Gandhi returned to India he had the prestige of a leader.

Since the beginning of the century the movement for Indian independence had been steadily gaining ground, Thirty years before, a few broadminded Englishmen, among whom were A. O. Hume and Sir William Wedderburn, had organized a National Indian Congress. Victorian Liberals, they had given the Congress a loyalist stamp and had tried to consolidate India's claims with the demands of England's sovereignty. In the meantime, however, Japan's victory over Russia had awakened the pride of Asiatic peoples, and Indian patriots resented Lord Curzon's provocative attitude. An extremist party was formed in the heart of the Congress, and its more aggressive nationalism corresponded to a general sentiment throughout the country. Until the war of 1914, however, the old constitutional part remained under the leadership of G. K. Gokhale, who was a great Indian patriot, although he believed in loyalty to England.

Although the Indian Congress, reflecting general sentiment, was in favor of home rule, or *Swaraj*, the various members disagreed as to the form this home rule should take. Some members believed in cooperation with England; others wanted to drive the English out of India. Some advocated the dominion system, as in Canada, while others asserted that India should aspire to become an independent nation like Japan. Gandhi proposed a solution. It was religious rather than political, but at bottom it was more radical than any of the others. The principles are to be found in his "Hind Swaraj." But as this solution was based on conditions in South Africa, Gandhi realized it would have to be modified to suit conditions in India. He also realized that while his stay in South Africa had made him unfamiliar with conditions in India, it had proved what an irresistible weapon *ahimsa*, non-violence, could be. And he determined, therefore, to study conditions in India in order to adapt the weapon of *ahimsa* to them.[1]

At this time Gandhi felt no antagonism for England. On the contrary, when the war broke out in 1914, he went to London to organize an Indian ambulance corps. As he explained in a letter written in 1921, he honestly believed himself a citizen of the empire. He refers to his attitude again and again, as in his letter addressed to "Every Englishman in India," published in 1920. No Englishman, he says, served the Government more faithfully than he during twenty-nine years of public life. He risked his life four times for England, and until 1919 he sincerely believed in cooperating with the Government. But now he can do so no longer.

Gandhi was not the only one to experience this change of feeling. In 1914 all India had been carried away by the hypocritical idealism of the so-called "war for justice." In asking for India's support the English Government had held out the most

1. Shortly before he died, Gokhale, Gandhi's beloved master, had suggested that Gandhi make a trip through India and study conditions at first hand, before going into politics. And Gandhi had promised not to take an active part in the political life of India for a year.

brilliant hopes. The granting of home rule, which the people longed for, was said to depend on India's attitude in the war. In August, 1917, the clever Indian secretary, E. S. Montagu, promised India a government responsible to the people. A consultation took place, and in July, 1918, the viceroy, Lord Chelmsford, and Mr. Montagu signed an official report recommending constitutional reform in India. The Allied armies were in a most precarious position in the early days of 1918. On April 2 Lloyd George had sent an appeal to the people of India, while the war conference, sitting at Delhi in the end of the same month, had hinted that the hour of India's independence was near. And India had replied as one man while Gandhi promised England his loyal backing. India contributed 985,000 men and made tremendous sacrifices. And she waited confidently for the promised reward.

The awakening was terrible. Danger was over in the end of 1918, and gone was the memory of services rendered. After the signing of the armistice the Government saw no reason for feigning any longer. Instead of granting the promised liberties, it suspended whatever freedom already existed. The Rowlatt bills, proposed at the Imperial Legislative Council at Delhi, expressed an insulting distrust of the country which had given so many proofs of its loyalty. These bills aimed to establish definitively the provisions of the Defense Act imposed on India dining the war, and made secret police services, censorship, and all the tyrannical annoyances of a real state of siege into a permanent reality. There was one burst of indignation all over India. The revolt began.[1] Gandhi led it.

1. The Satyagraha movement may be said to have begun February 28, 1919.

Hitherto Gandhi had been interested in social reforms only, devoting himself particularly to the conditions of agricultural workers. At Kaira, in the Gujarat, and at Champaran, in Behar, he had almost unnoticeably and with success tried out the formidable weapon which he was soon to use in national struggles. This weapon was the will of active passionate non-resistance. We will study it later under the name of *Satyagraha*, which Gandhi has given it.

Until 1919, however, Gandhi did not participate actively in the Indian nationalist movement. Having been united in 1916 by Mrs. Annie Besant, the most advanced elements soon outdistanced her and rallied under the leadership of the great Hindu, Lokamanya Bal Gangadhar Tilak, a man of extraordinary energy, uniting, as in a triple sheaf of iron, a great mind, a strong will, and a high character. His intelligence was perhaps even keener than Gandhi's, or, rather, it was more solidly nourished on old Asiatic culture. He was an erudite, a mathematician, who had sacrificed all personal ambitions to serve his country. Like Gandhi, he sought no personal recognition and longed only for the triumph of his ideal in order to be able to retire from the political field and go back to his scientific work. As long as he lived he was the undisputed leader of India. Who can say what would have happened if he had not met with an untimely death in 1920? If Tilak had lived, Gandhi, who revered Tilak's genius, while differing radically from him in regard to methods and policies, would no doubt have remained religious leader of the movement. How magnificently the people of India could have marched on under such a double leadership! They would have been irresistible, for Tilak was a master of action, just as Gandhi is a master of spiritual power. But fate decided otherwise. It is, perhaps, to be regretted, not only for Tilak's sake, but for India's and even for Gandhi's. The rôle of minority leader, of leader of the moral élite, would have been more in accordance with Gandhi's inmost desires and nature. He would have been happy to let Tilak rule the majority, for Gandhi never had any faith in majorities. But Tilak had. Tilak, a born mathematician and master of action, believed in numbers. He was democratic instinctively. He was resolutely a politician, who left religious considerations aside. He claimed that politics were not for *sadhus* (saints, pious men). This austere scientist would have sacrificed truth to patriotism. And this scrupulously honest and upright man, whose personal life was one of spotless purity, did not hesitate to say that in politics everything is justified. It might be said that Tilak's conception of politics and that of the dictators of Moscow have something in common. Not so with Gandhi's ideal.[1] Tilak's and Gandhi's discussions brought out their different points of view. Between men as sincere as they there is bound to be irreconcilable opposition, since their methods are based on their convictions, which are in fundamental opposition. Each man respected and revered the other. But Gandhi felt that if it came to the point he would always set truth first before liberty and even before his country, whereas Tilak set his country above everything. Gandhi feels that no matter how great his love for his country may be, his faith in his ideal, in religion as expressed in Truth, is greater still.

As he says on August 11,1920:

> I am wedded to India because I believe absolutely that she has a mission for the world... My religion has no geographical limits. I have a living faith in it which will transcend even my love for India herself.[2]

---

1. Gandhi explained his attitude toward Bolshevism on November 24, 1921.
2. August 11, 1920: Gandhi protests against the doctrine of the sword.

These noble words give the key to the struggle which we now will describe. They prove that the Apostle of India is the Apostle of the World, and that he is one of us. The battle the Mahatma began fighting four years ago is our battle.[1]

---

1. "Humanity is one. There are different races, but the higher a race the greater its duties." ("Ethical Religion")

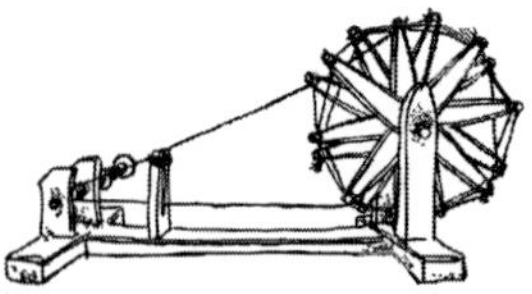

CHAPTER 5

It should be noted that when Gandhi stepped into the political field as leader of the opposition to the Rowlatt bills, he was moved only by a desire to spare the country from violence.[1] The revolt was bound to come; he knew there was no possibility of avoiding it. The point, therefore, was to turn it into non-violent channels.

To understand Gandhi's activity, it should be realized that his doctrine is like a huge edifice composed of two different floors or grades. Below is the solid groundwork, the basic foundation of religion. On this vast and unshakable foundation is based the political and social campaign. It is not the ideal continuation of the invisible foundation, but it is the best structure possible under present conditions. It is adapted to conditions.

In other words, Gandhi is religious by nature, and his doctrine is essentially religious. He is a political leader by necessity, because other leaders disappear, and the force of circumstances obliges him to pilot the ship through the storm and give practical political expression to his doctrine. These developments are interesting, but the essential part of the edifice is the crypt,

1. November 5, 1919.

which is deep and well built and meant to uphold a very different cathedral from the structure rapidly rising above it. The crypt alone is durable. The rest is temporary and only designed to serve during the transition years, until the plans for a cathedral worthy of the groundwork can be worked out. An understanding of the principles on which the vast subterranean crypt is based is essential, therefore, for here Gandhi's thought finds its real expression. It is into the depths of this crypt that he descends every day to seek inspiration and strength to carry on the work above.

Gandhi believes in the religion of his people, in Hinduism. But he is not a scholar, attached to the punctilious interpretation of texts, nor is he a blind believer accepting unquestioningly all the traditions of his religion. His religion must satisfy his reason and correspond to the dictates of his conscience.

> I would not make a fetish of religion and condone evil in its sacred name.[1]
>
> My belief in the Hindu scripture does not require me to accept every word and every verse as divinely inspired. I decline to be bound by any interpretation however learned it may be if it is repugnant to reason or moral sense.[2]

Nor does he look upon Hinduism as the only religion, and this is a very important point.

> I do not believe in the exclusive divinity of the Vedas. I believe the Bible, the Koran and the Zend-Avesta to be as divinely inspired as the Vedas... Hinduism is not a missionary religion. In it there is room for the worship of

1. October 27, 1920.
2. October 6, 1921.

> all the prophets in the world... Hinduism tells everyone to worship God according to his own faith or *Dharma* and so it lives in peace with all religions.[1]

He sees the errors and vices that have crept into religion through the centuries, and he brands them, but he adds:

> I can no more describe my feeling for Hinduism than for my own wife. She moves me as no other woman in the world can. Not that she has no faults; I dare say, she has many more than I see myself. But the feeling of an indissoluble bond is there. Even so I feel about Hinduism with all its faults and limitations. Nothing elates me so much as the music of the Gitâ or the Ramayana by Tulasidas, the only two books in Hinduism I may be said to know. I know that vice is going on to-day in all the great Hindu shrines but I love them in spite of their failings. I am a reformer through and through. But my zeal never takes me to the rejection of any of the essential things of Hinduism.[2]

What are the essential things in which Gandhi believes? In an article written October 6,1921, Gandhi defines his conception of Hinduism:

1. He believes, he says, in the "Vedas, the Upanishads, the Puranas and all that goes by the name of Hindu scriptures." He believes, therefore, in *Avataras* and rebirth.

---

1. All religions are like different roads leading to the same goal. ("Hind Swaraj.") "All religions are founded on the same moral laws. My ethical religion is made up of laws which bind men all over the world." ("Ethical Religion.")
2. October 6, 1921.

2. He believes in the *Varnashrama Dharma*[1] or the "Discipline of the Castes," in a sense which he considers "strictly Vedic," but which may not correspond to the present "popular and crude sense."

3. He believes in the "protection of the cow in a much larger sense than the popular."

4. He does not "disbelieve in idol worship."

Every Occidental who reads Gandhi's "Credo" and stops at these lines is apt to feel that they reveal a mentality so different from ours and so far removed in time and space as to make comparison with our ideals impossible, owing to the lack of a common measure. But if he will read on, he will find, a few lines below, the following words, which express a doctrine more familiar to us:

> I believe implicitly in the Hindu aphorism that no one truly knows the *Shastras* who has not attained perfection in Innocence [*Ahimsa*], Truth [*Satya*], and Self-Control [*Brahma-Charya]* and who has not renounced all acquisition or possession of wealth.

Here the words of the Hindu join those of the Gospel. And Gandhi was aware of their similarity. To an English clergyman who asked him in 1920 which books had influenced him most, Gandhi replied, "The New Testament."[2]

The last words of Gandhi's "Ethical Religion" are a quotation from the New Testament,[3] and he claims that the revelation of

1. Etymologically, *varna*, color, class or caste; *ashrama*, place of discipline; *dharma*, religion. Society, in other words, stands for "discipline of the castes."
2. February 25, 1920. In a second line Gandhi adds, "Ruskin and Tolstoi."
3. "Seek the Kingdom of God and His righteousness and all these things shall be added unto you."

passive resistance came to him after reading the Sermon on the Mount in 1893.[1] When the clergyman asked him, in surprise, if he had not found the same message in Hindu scriptures, Gandhi replied that while he has found inspiration and guidance in the Bhagavad Gitâ, which he reveres and admires, the secret of passive resistance was made clear to him through the New Testament. A great joy welled up in him, he says, when the revelation came to him, and again when the Gitâ confirmed this revelation.[2] Gandhi also says that Tolstoi's ideal, that the kingdom of God is within us, helped him mold his own faith into a real doctrine.[3]

It should not be forgotten that this Asiatic believer has translated Ruskin[4] and Plato[5] and quotes Thoreau, admires Mazzini, reads Edward Carpenter, and that he is, in short, familiar with the best that Europe and America have produced.

1. "Young India," February 25, 1920.
2. He says to Joseph J. Doke in 1908 that God has been incarnate throughout the ages, in different forms, because, as explained in the Gitâ, Krishna says: "When religion falls into decadence and unbelief prevails, I manifest myself. For the protection of all that is good, and the destruction of all that is evil, for the establishment of Dharma, I must be born and reborn, forever and ever." Christianism is part of Gandhi's theology. Christ is a radiant revelation of God. But not the only revelation. He is not seated on the throne alone.
3. The "Hind Swaraj" contains a list of about sixty of Tolstoi's works which Gandhi recommends to his followers, among them, "The Kingdom of God Is within You, What Is Art?" and "What Shall We Do?" He tells Joseph Doke that Tolstoi influenced him deeply, but that he does not agree with Tolstoi's political ideals. To a question asked him in 1921 as to his feeling for and opinion of Count Tolstoi, Gandhi replies (in "Young India" of October 25, 1921), "My relation to him was that of a devoted admirer who owes him much in life."
4. He was particularly fond of Ruskin's "Crown of Wild Olives."
5. "Apologia and Death of Socrates," translated by Gandhi, was one of the books confiscated by the Indian Government in 1919.

There is no reason why a Westerner should not understand Gandhi's doctrine as well as Gandhi understands those of our great men, provided the Westerner will take the trouble to study Gandhi a little deeply. It is true that the mere words of Gandhi's creed may surprise him, and that two paragraphs, in fact, if read superficially, may seem so different from our mentality as to form an almost insurmountable barrier between the religious ideals of Asia and Europe. One of these paragraphs refers to cow-protection and the other to the caste system. As for Gandhi's reference to idol-worship, it requires no special study. Gandhi explains his attitude when he says that he has no veneration for idols but believes idol-worship to be part of human nature. He considers it inherent to the frailty of the human mind, because we all "hanker after symbolism" and must needs materialize our faith in order really to understand it. When Gandhi says he does not disbelieve in idol-worship, he means no more than what we countenance in all our ritualistic churches of the West.

"Cow-protection," says Gandhi, is the central fact of Hinduism. He looks upon it as one of the "most wonderful phenomena of human evolution." Why? Because the cow, to him, is taken as the symbol of the entire "sub-human world." Cow-protection means that man concludes a pact of alliance with his dumb brethren; it signifies fraternity between man and beast. According to Gandhi's beautiful expression, by learning to respect, revere, an animal, man is "taken beyond his species and is enjoined to realize his identity with all that lives."

If the cow was selected in preference to other creatures it was because in India the cow was the best companion, the giver of plenty. Not only did she give the milk but she made agriculture possible. And Gandhi sees in "this gentle animal" a "poem of pity."

But there is nothing idolatrous about Gandhi's cow-worship, and no one condemns more harshly than he the fetishism of many so-called believers, who observe the letter of "cow-worship" without exercising a spirit of compassion "for the dumb creatures of God." Whoever understands the spirit of compassion and fellow-feeling that Gandhi would have men feel for their dumb brethren,—and who would have understood this better than the *poverello* Assisi?—is not surprised that Gandhi lays such stress on cow-protection in his creed. From this point of view he is quite justified in saying that cow-protection is the "gift of Hinduism to the world." To the precept of the gospel, "Love thy neighbor as thyself," Gandhi adds, "And every living being is thy neighbor."[1]

Gandhi's belief in the caste system is almost more difficult for a European or Western mind to understand—it seems more foreign, almost, than the idea of the fellowship of all living beings. I should perhaps say "European or Western mind of to-day," for while we still believe in a certain equality, Heaven knows how we will feel in the future, when we become thoroughly imbued with the consequences of the evolution, democratic in name only, which we are undergoing! I do not imagine that at our present stage of development my explanation of Gandhi's views will make them seem acceptable as regards the caste system; nor am I anxious to have them seem so. But I would like to make it clear that Gandhi's conception of the caste system is different from what we usually mean by that term, since he does not base it on pride or vain notions of social superiority, but on duties.

1. In regard to cow-worship see "Young India," March 16, June 8, June 29, August 4, 1920, and May 18, October 6, 1921. In regard to castes see articles December 8, 1920, and October 6, 1921.

> I am inclined to think [he says] that the law of heredity is an eternal law, and that any attempt to alter it must lead to utter confusion... *Varnashrama* or the caste system, is inherent in human nature. Hinduism has simply reduced it to a science.

Gandhi believes in four classes or castes. The *Brahmans*, the intellectual and spiritual class; the military and governmental class; the *Vaishyas*, the commercial, industrial class; and the *Shudras*, manual workers and laborers. This classification does not imply any superiority or inferiority. It simply stands for different vocations. "These classes define duties, they confer no privileges."[1]

> It is against the genius of Hinduism to arrogate to oneself a higher status or assign others to a lower. All are born to serve God's creation, the *Brahman* with his knowledge, the *Kshatriya* with his power of protection, the *Vaishya* with his commercial ability, the *Shudra* with his bodily labor.
>
> This does not mean that a *Brahman* is absolved from bodily labor but it does mean that he is predominantly a man of knowledge and fittest by training and heredity to impart it to others. There is nothing again to prevent a *Shudra* from acquiring all the knowledge he wishes. Only he will best serve with his body and need not envy others their special qualities for service. A *Brahman* who claims superiority by right of knowledge falls and has no knowledge. Varnashrama is self-restraint and conservation of economy and energy...

1. This is in accordance with the Upanishads, for when the primitive classes hardened into proud castes, in the course of centuries, these Hindu scriptures express protest and disapproval.

Gandhi's caste system is based, therefore, on "abnegation and not on privileges." It should not be forgotten, moreover, that according to Hinduism reincarnation reestablishes a general equilibrium, as in the course of successive existences a *Brahman* becomes a *Shudra*, and *vice versa.*

The caste system, which deals with different classes of equal rank, bears no relation whatsoever to the attitude of Hindus to the "untouchables," or pariahs. We will study later on Gandhi's passionate appeals for the pariahs. His campaign in favor of the "suppressed classes" is one of the most appealing phases of his apostleship. Gandhi regards the pariah system as a blot on Hinduism; it is a vile deformation of the real doctrine, and he suffers intolerably by it.

> I would rather be torn to pieces than disown my brothers of the suppressed classes... I do not want to be reborn, but if I have to be reborn, I should be "untouchable" so that I may share their sorrows, sufferings and the affronts leveled at them in order that I may endeavor to free them from their miserable condition.

And he adopts a little "untouchable" girl and speaks with emotion of this charming little imp of seven who rules the household with her gay prattle.

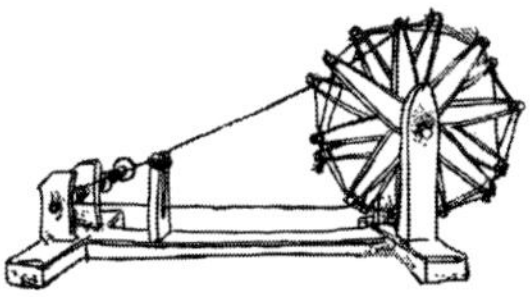

Chapter 6

I have said enough to show Gandhi's great evangelical heart beating under his Hindu creed. Gandhi is a Tolstoi in a more gentle, appeased, and, if I dared, I would say, in a more Christian sense, for Tolstoi is not so much a Christian by nature as by force of will.

The resemblance between the two men is greatest, or perhaps Tolstoi's influence has been strongest, in their condemnation of European and Occidental civilization.

Ever since Rousseau our Western civilization has been attacked by the freest and broadest minds of Europe. When Asia began to wake to a realization of her own power and revolt against Western oppression, she had only to peer into Europe's own files to compile formidable records of the iniquity of her so-called civilized invaders. Gandhi did not fail to do so, and in his "Hind Swaraj" he cites a list of books, many of which were written by Englishmen, condemning European civilization. But the document to which there can be no rejoinder is that which Europe herself has traced in the lifeblood of races oppressed and despoiled in the name of lying principles and, above all, in the brazen revelation of Europe's lies, greed, and ferocity as unfolded during the last war, called the "War for Civilization." And in it Europe sank to such depths that in her insanity she even invited the peoples of Asia and Africa to contemplate her nudity. They saw her and judged her.

> The last war has shown as nothing else has the Satanic[1] nature of the civilization that dominates Europe to-day. Every canon of public morality has been broken by the victors in the name of virtue. No lie has been considered too foul to be uttered. The motive behind every crime is not religious or spiritual but grossly material... Europe to-day is only nominally Christian. In reality it is worshipping Mammon.[2]

You will find sentiments such as these expressed again and again, during the last five years, both in India and Japan. Leaders too prudent to voice them openly show by their attitude that such is their inmost conviction. This is not the least disastrous result of the Pyrrhic victory of 1918.

Gandhi, however, had seen the real face of Western civilization long before 1914. It had revealed itself to him unmasked during his twenty years' campaign in South Africa, and in 1908, in his "Hind Swaraj," he calls modern civilization the "great vice."

Civilization, says Gandhi, is civilization in name only. In reality it corresponds to what ancient Hinduism called the dark ages. It has set material well-being up as the only goal of life. It scorns spiritual values. It maddens Europeans, leads them to worship money only, and prevents them from finding peace or

1. A term often used by Gandhi. "Untouchability is an invention of Satan." (June 19, 1921.)
2. September 8, 1920.

cultivating the best within them. Civilization in the Western sense means hell for the weak and for the working classes. It saps the vitality of the race. But this Satanic civilization will destroy itself. Western civilization is India's real enemy, much more than the English, who, individually, are not bad, hut simply suffer from their civilization. Gandhi criticizes those of his compatriots who would want to drive out the English, to develop India themselves, and civilize her according to European standards. This, he says, would be like having the nature of a tiger without the tiger. India's aim should be to repudiate Western civilization.

In his arraignment of Western civilization Gandhi scores three categories of men particularly: magistrates, doctors, and teachers.

Gandhi's objection to teachers is quite comprehensible, since they have brought the Hindus up to scorn or neglect their own language and to disown their real aspirations; in fact, the teachers in India have inflicted a sort of national degradation on the schoolchildren in their charge. Besides, Western teachers appeal to the mind only; they neglect the education of the heart and of the character. Finally, they depreciate bodily labor, and to spread a purely literary education in a country where eighty per cent of the population is agricultural and ten per cent industrial is positively criminal.

The profession of magistrate is immoral. In India the courts are an instrument of British domination; they encourage dissensions among Indians, and in a general way they foster and increase misunderstanding and animosity. They stand for a fattening, lucrative exploitation of the worst instincts.

As for the medical profession, Gandhi admits he was attracted to it at first, but he soon realized it was not honorable.

For Western medical science is concerned with giving relief to suffering bodies only. It does not strive to do away with the cause of suffering and disease, which, as a rule, is nothing but vice. In fact, Western medical science may almost be said to encourage vice by making it possible for a man to satisfy his passions and appetites at the least possible risk. It contributes, therefore, to demoralize people; it weakens their will-power by helping them to cure themselves with "black magic" prescriptions instead of forcing them to strengthen their character by disciplinary rules for body and soul.[1] In opposition to the false medical science of the West, which Gandhi has often criticized unfairly, he places preventive medical science. He has written a little pamphlet on the subject entitled "A Guide to Health," which is the fruit of twenty years' experience. It is a moral as well as a therapeutic treatise, for, according to Gandhi, "disease is the result of our thoughts as much as of our acts." He considers it a relatively simple matter to establish certain rules that will prevent disease. For all disease springs from the same origin, i. e., from neglect of the natural laws of health. The body is God's dwelling-place. It must be kept pure. There is truth in Gandhi's point of view, but he refuses a little too obstinately to recognize the efficacy of remedies that have really proved to be useful. His moral precepts are also extremely rigid.[2]

---

1. It should not be forgotten that one of Gandhi's main arguments against the medical science of Europe is its use of vivisection, which he brands as "man's blackest crime."
2. Particularly in regard to sexual relations. Gandhi's doctrine resembles that of St. Paul in its rigorism.

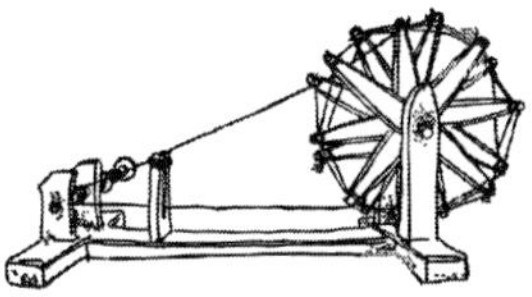

CHAPTER 7

But the nucleus of modern civilization, its heart, so to speak, is machinery. Age of iron! Heart of iron! The machine has become a monstrous idol. It must be done away with. Gandhi's most ardent desire is to see machinery wiped out of India. To a free India, heir to British machinery, he would prefer an India dependent on the British market. It would be better to buy materials manufactured in Manchester than to set up Manchester factories in India. An Indian Rockefeller would be no better than a European capitalist. Machinery is the great sin which enslaves nations, and money is a poison as much as sexual vice.

Indian progressives, however, imbued with modern ideas, ask what would become of India if she were to have no railroads, tramways, or industries? To this Gandhi asks if India did not exist before they were invented? For thousands of years India has resisted, alone, unshaken, the changing flood of empires. Everything else has passed. But thousands of years ago India learned the art of self-control and mastered the science of happiness. She has nothing to learn from other nations. She does not need the machinery of large cities. Her ancient prosperity was founded on the plow and the spinning-wheel, and on a knowledge of Hindu philosophy.

India must go back to the sources of her ancient culture. Not all at once, of course, but gradually. And every one must help in the evolution.[1]

This is Gandhi's fundamental argument. It is a very important one, and demands discussion. For it stands for a denial of progress and, virtually, of Europe's scientific achievement.[2] This medieval conception is apt, therefore, to clash with the volcanic forward march of the human mind and incurs the risk of being blown to bits. But, first of all, it would perhaps be wiser to say, the "forward march of a certain *phase* of the human mind," for if one may believe, as I believe, in the symphonic unity of the universal spirit, one must realize that it is made up of many different voices, each one singing its own part. Our youthful Occident carried away by its own score, does not realize sufficiently that it has not always led the song, nor that its own law of progress is subject to eclipses, backslidings, and recommencements; that the history of human civilization is really a history of human civilizations, and that while within the domain of each civilization a certain progress may be discernible, a progress irregular, chaotic, broken, and at times completely halted, it would be wrong to say that the predominance of one great civilization over another necessarily implies general human progress.

But without entering into a discussion as to the European dogma of progress and merely bearing in mind that this dogma,

---

1. "Hind Swaraj."
2. Although Gandhi does not approve of European science, he realizes the necessity of scientific achievement. He admires the disinterested zeal and the spirit of self-sacrifice of European men of science and frequently calls their abnegation greater than that of Hindu believers. But he disapproves the goal they are pursuing even though he admires their state of mind. There is an evident antagonism between Gandhi and European science. And in this connection we will see, later on, how Tagore protests against Gandhi's medievalism.

such as it is, conflicts with Gandhi's faith, we must realize that no conflict will weaken Gandhi's faith. To believe anything else would be to show a total ignorance of the workings of the Oriental mind. As Gobineau says: "Asiatics are much more obstinate than we, in every way. They will wait centuries, if necessary, for the fulfilment of their ideal, and when it rises triumphant after such a long slumber it does not seem to have aged or lost any of its vitality." Centuries mean nothing to a Hindu. Gandhi is prepared for the triumph of his cause within the year. But he is equally prepared for it within the course of several centuries. He does not force time. And if time makes haste slowly, he regulates his gait by its march.

If, therefore, in the course of his campaign Gandhi finds India insufficiently prepared to understand and practice the radical reforms he wishes to impose, he will adapt his doctrine to conditions. He will bide his time. That is why it is not astonishing to hear the irreconcilable enemy of machinery declare, in 1921:

> I would not weep over the disappearance of machinery or consider this a calamity. But for the time being I have no designs on machinery as such.[1]

Or:

> The law of complete Love is the Law of my being. But I am not preaching this final law through the political measures I advocate. I know that any such attempt is foredoomed to failure. To expect a whole mass of men and women to obey that law all at once is not to know it's

1. January 19, 1921.

working.[1] I am not a visionary. I claim to be a practical idealist.[2]

Gandhi never asks men for more than they can give. But he asks for all that they can give. And this is much in a nation like India—a formidable nation, through its numerical power, its force of duration, and its abysmal soul. From the very first Gandhi and India have formed a pact; they understand each other without words. Gandhi knows what he can demand of India, and India is prepared to give whatever Gandhi may demand.

Between Gandhi and India there reigns, first of all, absolute agreement as to goal: *Swaraj*, home rule, for the nation.[3]

"I know," he says, "that *Swaraj* is the object of the nation and not non-violence."

And he adds—words amazing on his lips, "I would rather see India freed by violence than enchained like a slave to her foreign oppressors."

But, he continues, correcting himself at once, this is an impossible supposition, for violence can never free India. *Swaraj* can only be attained by soul-force. This is India's real weapon, the invincible weapon of love and truth. Gandhi expresses it by the term *Satyagraha*, which he defines as truth-force and love-force.[4] Gandhi's genius revealed itself when, by the preaching of

1. March 9, 1920.
2. August 11, 1920.
3. Etymology: *Swa*, self; *raj*, government, autonomy. The word is as old as the Vedas, but it was adopted by Dadabhai, Gandhi's Parsee master, who made it part of the political vocabulary.
4. Etymology: *Satya*, just right; *Agraha*, attempt, effort. Hence, *Satyagraha*, a just effort, in the sense of meaning non-acceptation of or resistance to injustice.

this gospel, he revealed to his people their real nature and their hidden strength.

Gandhi used the word *Satyagraha* in South Africa to explain the difference between his ideal and that of passive resistance. Particular stress must be laid on the difference between these two movements. Nothing is more false than to call Gandhi's campaign a movement of passive resistance. No one has a greater horror of passivity than this tireless fighter, who is one of the most heroic incarnations of a man who *resists*. The soul of his movement is active resistance—resistance which finds outlet, not in violence, but in the active force of love, faith and sacrifice. This threefold energy is expressed in the word *Satyagraha.*

Let not the coward try to hide his cowardice under Gandhi's banner! Gandhi drives him out of the community. Better violence than cowardice!

> Where there is only a choice between cowardice and violence I advise violence...[1] I cultivate the quiet courage of dying without killing. But to him who has not this courage I advise that of killing and of being killed, rather than that of shamefully fleeing from danger. For he who runs away commits mental violence; he runs away because he has not the courage to be killed while he kills.[2]
>
> I would risk violence a thousand times rather than emasculation of the race.[3] I would rather have India resort to arms to defend her honor than that she should

Gandhi defines it, November 5, 1919, as meaning "holding on to truth, hence, truth-force." And he adds, "I have also defined it as love-force or soul-force."

1. August 11, 1920.
2. October 20, 1921.
3. August 4, 1920.

in a cowardly manner become or remain a helpless victim to her own dishonor.[1]

But I believe that non-violence is infinitely superior to violence, forgiveness more manly than punishment. Forgiveness adorns a soldier. Abstinence is forgiveness only when there is power to punish; it is meaningless when it pretends to proceed from a helpless creature... I do not believe India to be helpless. One hundred thousand Englishmen need not frighten three hundred million human beings.

Besides.

Strength does not come from physical capacity. It comes from an indomitable will. Non-violence does not mean meek submission to the will of the evil-doer but the putting of one's whole soul against the will of the tyrant. Working under this law of our being it is possible for a single individual to defy the whole might of an unjust empire and lay the foundation for that empire's fall or its regeneration.

But at the cost of what? Of *suffering*—the *great law.*

Suffering is the mark of the human tribe. It is an eternal law.[2] The mother suffers so that her child may live. Life comes out of death. The condition of wheat growing is that the seed grain should perish. No country has ever risen

1. August 11, 1920. One of the rules of the *Satayagraha Ashram*, the school founded by Gandhi, is "absence of fear." The spirit must be freed from fear of kings, nations, castes, family, men, wild beasts, and death. It is also the fourth condition of non-violent resistance in the Hindra. The others are chastity, poverty, and truth.

2. June 16, 1920.

> without being purified through the fire of suffering... It is impossible to do away with the law of suffering which is the one indispensable condition of our being. Progress is to be measured by the amount of suffering undergone... the purer the suffering, the greater is the progress.[1]
>
> Non-violence in its dynamic condition means conscious suffering... I have ventured to place before India the ancient law of self-sacrifice, the law of suffering. The *Rishis* who discovered the law of non-violence in the midst of violence were greater geniuses than Newton, greater warriors than Wellington. Having themselves known the use of arms they realized their uselessness and taught a weary world that salvation lay not through violence but through non-violence... The religion of non-violence is not meant merely for the *Rishis* and saints. It is meant for the common people as well. Non-violence is the law of our species as violence is the law of the brute. The dignity of man requires obedience to a higher law—to the strength of the spirit... I want India to practice non-violence being conscious of her strength and power. I want India to recognize that she has a soul that cannot perish and that can rise triumphant above every physical weakness and defy the physical combination of a whole world.[2]

Exalted pride, his proud love of India, demands she should scorn violence as unworthy and be ready to sacrifice herself. Non-violence is her title of nobility. If she abandons it she falls. Gandhi cannot bear the thought.

---

1. August 11, 1920.
2. April 6, 1921.

> If India made violence her creed I would not care to live in India. She would cease to evoke any pride in me. My patriotism is subservient to my religion. I cling to India like a child to its mother's breast because I feel that she gives me the spiritual nourishment I need. If she were to fail me, I would feel like an orphan, without hope of ever finding a guardian. Then the snow altitudes of the Himalayas must give what rest they can to my bleeding soul...[1]

1. A few months before his imprisonment Gandhi replies to the criticisms as to "illogic" of his conduct. His critics jeer at the assistance he tendered England in South Africa and during the World War. Gandhi, in replying, does not try to evade the issue. He honestly believed, he says, that he was a citizen of the empire; it was not his business to judge the Government. He would consider it wrong for every man to look upon himself as justified in criticizing the Government. He had confidence in England's wisdom and loyalty as long as possible. The Government's aberration has destroyed his faith in it. Let the Government take the consequences! (November 17, 1921.)

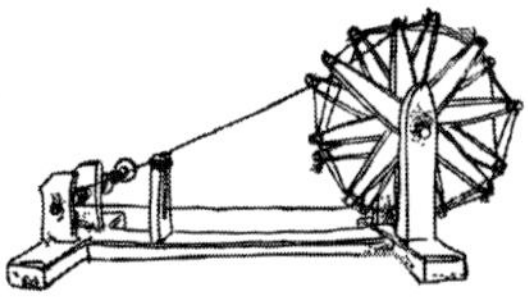

CHAPTER 8

But Gandhi does not doubt India's endurance. In February, 1919, he decided to start the *Satyagraha* movement, whose efficacy had already been tested during the agrarian revolt in 1918.

The campaign is not at all political, as yet: Gandhi is still a loyalist. And he remains one as long as he retains a grain of faith in England's loyalty. Until January, 1920, he advocated cooperation with the empire, even though the nationalists criticized him bitterly therefore.[1] Gandhi's arguments are inspired by his sincere conviction, and during the first year of his campaign against the Government he could truthfully assure Lord Hunter that he believed the disciples of *Satyagraha* to be the most loyal supporters of the Constitution. Only the narrow-minded obstinacy of the Government forced India's moral guide finally to tear up the contract of loyalty by which he considered himself hound.

To begin with, therefore, the *Satyagraha* campaign takes the form of constitutional opposition to the Government. It is a respectful appeal for certain urgent reforms. The Government is guilty of passing an unjust law. The *Satyagrahi*, who are

1. April 6, 1921.

law-abiding people, will disobey this law deliberately, because they consider it unjust. If their attitude does not convince the Government of the necessity of repealing the law, they will extend their disobedience to other laws, and eventually they may cease all cooperation with the Government. But how different is the meaning which India gives to this word from that which we in the West give to it! Such extraordinary religious heroism as is contained in it!

As the *Satyagrahi* are not allowed to use violence in advancing their cause (the idea being that the adversary, too, is sincere, since what seems truth to one person may seem untruth to another, while violence never carries conviction),[1] they must rely solely on the love-force that radiates from their faith and on their willingness to accept suffering and sacrifice joyously, freely.[2] This constitutes irresistible propaganda. With it the cross of Christ and his little flock conquered the Roman Empire.

In order to emphasize the religious character of the people's willingness to sacrifice themselves for the eternal ideals of justice and liberty, the Mahatma inaugurated the movement by setting April 6, 1919,[3] aside as a day of prayers and fasting, by imposing a *hartal* of all India.[4] This was the first step.

---

1. On the contrary, violence degrades the person who makes use of it. The Allies' violence made them like unto the Germans, whose acts they flayed, in the beginning of the war. (June 9, 1920.)
2. The hardest fiber must melt in the fire of love. If it does not melt it is because the fire is not strong enough. (March 9, 1920.) Those joining the *Satyagraha* movement had to promise to disobey the laws declared by the *Satyagraha* committee to be unjust, to follow in the path of truth, and to abstain from all violence against the lives, persons, or property of their adversaries.
3. March 23, 1919.
4. This Hindustani word of Mohammedan origin means cessation of work.

This first step went right to the heart of the people, stirred their inmost consciousness. For the first time all classes of India united in the same ideal. India found herself.

Order reigned everywhere. At Delhi only there were a few disturbances.[1] Gandhi set out to quiet them. But the Government had him arrested and sent him back to Bombay. The news of his arrest caused riots in Punjab; at Amritsar some houses were looted, and a few people were killed. In the night of April 11 General Dyer arrived with his troops and occupied the city. Order reigned everywhere. The fifteenth was a great Hindu feast-day. A meeting was to take place at an open space called Jallianwalla Bagh. The crowd was peaceful and numbered many women and children. The night before General Dyer had sent out an order forbidding public meetings, but no one had heard about it. The general, however, came to Jallianwalla Bagh with his machine-guns and without warning opened fire on the defenseless mass of people. The firing lasted about ten minutes, till the ammunition was used up. As the grounds were surrounded by high walls, no one could escape. From five to six hundred Hindus were killed, and a much larger number wounded. There was no one to care for the dead and wounded. As the result of the massacre, martial law was proclaimed, and a reign of terror spread over Punjab. Aëroplanes threw bombs on the unarmed crowds. The most honorable citizens were dragged to court, flogged, and forced to crawl on their knees, and subjected to the most shocking indignities. It was as if a wind of madness swept over the English rulers. It was as if the law of non-violence, proclaimed by India, stirred European violence to frenzy. Gandhi saw bloodshed and suffering were ahead. But he had not promised to lead his people

1. Delhi, incidentally, made a mistake in the date of the *hartal* and celebrated it March 30.

to victory along a white road. He had warned them that the path would be washed with blood. Jallianwalla Bagh was only the beginning:

> We must be prepared to contemplate with equanimity not a thousand murders of innocent men and women but many thousands before we attain a status in the world that shall not be surpassed by any nation... We hope, therefore, that all concerned will take rather than lose heart and treat hanging as an ordinary affair of life.[1]

Owing to the rigorous military censorship, the news of the horrors of Punjab did not leak out for several months. But when it did leak out[2] a wave of indignation swept over India and alarmed even English opinion. An investigation was ordered, and Lord Hunter presided over the commission.

In the meantime, the National Indian Congress formed a subcommission to carry on investigations independently of the Government, but along the same lines. It was to the obvious interest of the Government, as all intelligent Englishmen realized, to punish those guilty of the massacre of Amritsar. Gandhi did not demand as much as that. In his admirable moderation he did not ask for the punishment of General Dyer and the guilty officers. While denouncing them, he felt no bitterness and sought no vengeance. One bears no ill will to a madman. But one must put him where he can do no damage. Gandhi, therefore, merely asked that General Dyer be recalled. But *quos vult perdere...* Before the results of the investigation could be published, the Government passed an indemnity act to protect

---

1. April 7, 1920.
2. Gandhi, to quiet the effervescence instead of trying to exploit it as an ordinary revolutionary leader would have done, suspended the movement on April 18.

official employees. Though Dyer was removed from his post, he was rewarded with money contributed from private sources.

While India was still in effervescence after the Punjab affair, a second conflict arose between the Government and the people, a more serious one this time, because it implied a flagrant violation of solemn promises. The Government's attitude shattered whatever confidence India still had in the good faith of the English rulers, and brought on the great revolt.

The European War had placed the Moslems of India in a very painful dilemma. They were torn between their duty as loyal citizens of the empire and faithful followers of their religious chief. They agreed to help England when she promised not to attack the sultan's or the caliph's sovereignty. It was the sense of Moslem opinion in India that the Turks should remain in Turkey in Europe and that the sultan should retain not only authority over the Holy Places of Islam, but over Arabia as delimited by Mohammedan scholars with the enclaves of Mesopotamia, Syria, and Palestine. This Lloyd George and the viceroy solemnly promised. When the war was over, however, all pledges were forgotten. And when the rumors of the peace terms to be imposed on Turkey began to circulate in 1919, the Moslems in India began to grow restless, and their discontent finally started the Khilafat or Califat movement.

It began October 17,1919 (Khilafat day), with an imposing peaceful demonstration, which was followed, about a month later (November 24), by the opening of an All-India Khilafat Conference at Delhi. Gandhi presided. With his quick glance he had realized that the Islamic agitation might be made into the instrument of Indian unity. The problem of uniting the various races in India was a most difficult one. The English had always taken advantage of the natural enmity between Hindus and Moslems;

Gandhi even accuses them of having fostered it. At any rate, they had never tried to conciliate the two peoples, who challenged each other childishly. To annoy the Mohammedans, for instance, the Hindus used to make a point of singing when they passed the mosques where silence should reign, while the Mohammedans lost no opportunity of jeering the Hindus' cow-worship. Mutual ill will and persistent animosity reigned between the two races, who never associated with each other and were not allowed to intermarry or even eat in common. The English Government rested sweetly on the cushion of implicit trust in the impossibility of the two ever agreeing and adopting a common policy. When Gandhi's voice, therefore, proclaimed the identity of the Hindu and the Moslem cause, it awoke with a start. In an outburst of generosity, which happened to be sound politics, Gandhi urged the Hindus to do all in their power to advance Mohammedan claims.

> Hindus, Parsees, Christians, or Jews, if we wish to live as one nation, the interest of any one of us must be the interest of all. The only deciding consideration can be the justice of a particular cause.

Mohammedan blood had already mixed with that of the Hindus in the tragic massacre of Amritsar. The two people now had to seal their alliance, an unconditional alliance. The Moslems were the most advanced and audacious element in India. And they were the first to announce, at this Khilafat Conference, that they would refuse to cooperate with the Government if their demands were not met. Gandhi approved of this measure, but in his innate horror of going to extremes he refused at the time to advocate the boycott of British goods, for he looked upon the boycott as an expression of weakness or thirst for vengeance.

A second Khilafat Conference met at Amritsar in the end of December, 1919, and decided to send a deputation to Europe to inform the English Government and the Supreme Council of India's attitude. It also voted for the sending of an ultimatum to the viceroy, warning him of trouble if the peace terms should prove unsatisfactory. Finally a third conference, meeting in Bombay in February, 1920, issued a manifesto which, in its violent arraignment of Great Britain's policy, was a forerunner of the coming storm.

Gandhi realized the storm was brewing, and instead of trying to call it forth he did all in his power to break its violence.

It seemed as if England also realized the danger. By belated concessions she seemed to be making desperate efforts to avert the consequences of her former attitude. An Indian Reform Act based on the Montagu-Chelmsford report gave the people in India more influence in the Central Government as well as in local administrations. The king approved the act by a proclamation of December 24, 1919, in which he invited the people of India and the functionaries to cooperate with the Government in every way, while he also urged the viceroy to pardon political offenses and recommended a general amnesty. Gandhi, always ready to believe in the adversary's good faith, interpreted these measures as signifying a sort of tacit agreement to deal more justly with India, and he called upon the people to welcome the reforms. He confessed that they were insufficient, but he said they should be accepted as the starting-point for greater victories. He urged the conference to approve them unreservedly. After a heated debate the National Indian Congress adopted his view.

But soon it became evident that Gandhi's hopes were built on illusions. The viceroy did not heed the king's appeal for clemency, and instead of setting prisoners free, the doors of the jails opened only for executions. It became evident that the promised reforms would remain inoperative.

On top of this came the news of the peace conditions imposed on Turkey, May 14, 1920. In a message to the people the viceroy admitted they would prove disappointing, but he advised the Moslems to resign themselves to the inevitable.

Then came the publication of the official report on the Amritsar massacres. It was the last straw.

India's national consciousness was aroused. All ties were broken.

The Khilafat Committee, meeting at Bombay, May 28, 1920, passed a resolution adopting Gandhi's non-cooperation policy, and this resolution was ratified unanimously by the Moslem Conference of Allahabad, June 80, 1920.

Gandhi, in the meantime, wrote an open letter to the viceroy informing him that the movement of non-cooperation would begin. He explained why he had recourse to it, and his arguments are worth studying, for they prove that even then Gandhi was hoping to avoid a break with England. In the bottom of his heart he still hoped that the Government might be brought to mend its ways by purely legal methods:

> The only course open to me is either in despair to sever all connection with British rule or, if I still retain faith in the inherent superiority of the British Constitution, to adopt such means as will rectify the wrong done and thus restore confidence. I have not lost faith in the superiority of the British Constitution and it is because I believe in it that I have advised my Moslem friends to withdraw their support from Your Excellency's Government, and advised the Hindus to join them.

And this noble citizen of the empire the blind pride of the empire spurned.

PART TWO

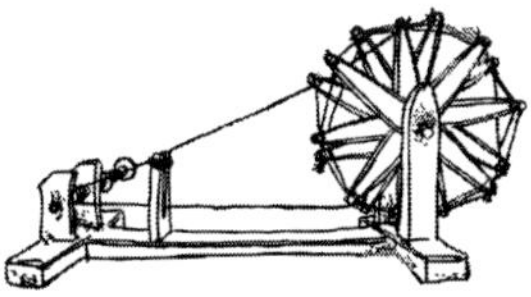

CHAPTER 1

On July 28, 1920, Gandhi announced that non-coöperation would be proclaimed August 1, and as a preparatory measure he ordered that a day of fasting and prayer be held the day before. He had no fear of governmental fury, but he feared the fury of the populace, and he bent every effort to have order and discipline reign within the Indian ranks. He declared:

> Effective non-coöperation depends upon complete organization. Disorderliness comes from anger. There must be no violence. Violence means retrogression in our case, and useless waste of innocent lives. Above everything else, there must be complete order.

The tactics of non-coöperation had been defined two months before by Gandhi and the committee of non-coöperation, and they included the following measures:

1. Surrender of all titles of honor and honorary offices.
2. Non-participation in government loans.
3. Suspension by lawyers of practice, and settlement of court disputes by private arbitration.
4. Boycott of government schools by children and parents.

5. Boycott of the reformed Councils.
6. Non-participation in government parties and other official functions.
7. Refusal to accept any civil or military post.
8. Agreements to spread the doctrine of Swadeshi.[1]

In other words, the negative part of the program should be completed by constructive measures, which would lead to the building up of the new India of the future.

This program specified the first steps to be taken, and we must admire the prudent sagacity of the leader who, after cranking up the enormous machine of Hindu revolt, stops it short, so to speak, and holds it back, pulsating, at the first turn, a method in startling opposition to that of our European revolutionaries. Gandhi is not planning civil disobedience for the present. He knows civil disobedience. He has studied it in Thoreau, whom he quotes in his articles, and he takes pains to explain the difference between it and non-coöperation. Civil disobedience, he says, is more than a mere refusal to obey the law. It means deliberate opposition to the law; it is an infraction of the law, and can be carried out only by an elite, while non-coöperation should be a mass movement. Gandhi means to prepare the masses in India for civil disobedience but they must be trained for it by a gradual process. He knows that at present people are not ripe for it, and he does not want to set them loose before he feels sure that they have mastered the art of self-control. So he launches

1. Etymologically, *swa*, self, oneself; *deshi*, country. Hence, national independence. The non-coöperators usually interpret it in the narrower sense of economic independence. It will be seen, further on, the sort of social gospel which Gandhi's followers make out of the idea. ("Gospel of Swadeshi.")

non-coöperation. Non-coöperation, in this first stage, does not include a refusal to pay taxes. Gandhi is biding his time.

August 1,1920, Gandhi gives the signal for the movement by his famous letter to the viceroy, surrendering his decorations and honorary titles:

> It is not without a pang that I return the Kaisar-i-Hind Gold Medal granted to me by your predecessor for my humanitarian work in South Africa, the Zulu War Medal, granted in South Africa for my services as officer in charge of the Indian Volunteer Ambulance Corps in 1906, and the Boer War Medal for my services as assistant superintendent of the Indian Volunteer Stretcher-bearer Corps during the Boer War of 1899-1900.

But, he adds, after referring to the scenes that took place in the Punjab and the events back of the Khilafat movement:

> I can retain neither respect nor affection for a Government which has been moving from wrong to wrong in order to defend its immorality... The Government must be moved to repentance.
>
> I have therefore ventured to suggest non-coöperation which enables those who wish to disassociate themselves from the Government and which, if unattended by violence, must compel the Government co retrace its steps and undo its wrongs.

And Gandhi expresses the hope that the viceroy will see his way to do justice, and that he will call a conference of the recognized leaders of the people, and consult with them.

Gandhi's example was immediately followed. Hundreds of magistrates sent in their resignations, thousands of students left the colleges, the courts were abandoned, the schools were emptied. The All-India Congress, meeting in special session in Calcutta in the beginning of September, approved Gandhi's decisions by an overwhelming majority. Gandhi and his friend Maulana Shaukat Ali toured the country and met with tremendous ovations everywhere.

Never did Gandhi show himself a greater leader than during the first year of his action. He had to hold back the violence that lay smoldering, ready to leap into flame at the slightest provocation. Gandhi fears and abhors mob violence more than anything else. He considers "mobocracy" the greatest danger that menaces India. He hates war, but would rather have it than the insane violence of *Caliban.* "If India has to achieve her freedom by violence, let it be by the disciplined violence named war," not by mob revolts. Gandhi looks with disfavor upon all demonstrations and mass-meetings, even in celebration of some joyous event, for out of a large crowd filled with noise and confusion frenzied violence may burst for no apparent reason. And he insists on the necessity of maintaining strict discipline. "We must evolve order out of chaos," he says, "introduce people's law instead of mob law." And the mystic with the clear, firm eyes, whose sound practical sense equals that of the great European mystics who founded religious orders and dominated the souls of men, gives precise, detailed rules as to how to canalize the torrents of popular meetings and demonstrations.

"One great stumbling-block," he says, speaking of the organization of mass-meetings, "is that we have neglected music. Music means rhythm, order. Unfortunately, in India, music has been the prerogative of the few. It has never become nationalized...

I would make compulsory a proper singing, in company, of national songs. And to that end I would have great musicians attending every congress or conference and teaching mass music. Nothing is so easy as to train mobs, for the simple reason that they have no mind, no meditation."

Gandhi makes a list of suggestions. No raw volunteers should be accepted to assist in the organization of the big demonstrations. None but the most experienced should be at the head. Volunteers should always have a general instruction-book on their persons. They should be dispersed among the crowd and should learn flag and whistle signaling to pass instructions. National cries should be fixed and raised at the right moment. Crowds should be prevented from entering the railroad stations; they should be taught to stand back and leave a clear passage in the streets for people and carriages. Little children should never be brought out in the crowds, etc.

In other words, Gandhi makes himself the orchestra leader of his oceans of men.[1]

---

1. September 8 and 24, October 20, 1920.

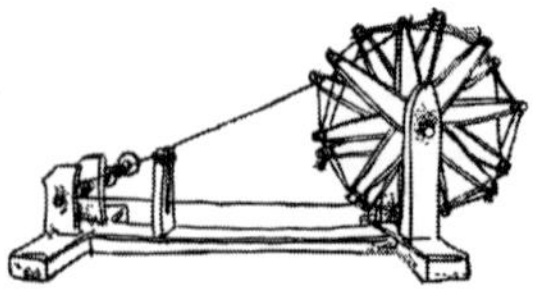

CHAPTER 2

But while the mob may break out into violence, unconsciously, blindly, moved by a sudden unreasonable impulse, there is a political faction which advocates violence deliberately and consciously. Many of the best men in India believe that national independence can be reached only by violent methods. This faction does not understand Gandhi's doctrine and does not believe in its political efficacy. It demands action, direct action. Gandhi receives anonymous letters urging him to stop advocating non-violence, and, worse, others implying cynically that his doctrine of non-violence is merely a mask and that the time has now come to throw it aside and give the signal for battle. Gandhi replies vehemently. He discusses the arguments passionately.[1] In a series of beautiful articles he censures the "doctrine of the sword." He denies that Hindu scriptures and the Koran approve violence. Violence is not part of the doctrine of any religion. Jesus is the prince of passive resistance. The Bhagavad Gitâ does not preach violence, but the fulfilment of duty even at the cost

1. August 11 and 25, 1920.

of one's life.[1] As man has not been given the power to create, he has not the right to destroy the smallest creature that lives. There must be no hatred for any one, not even for the evil-doer; but this does not mean that one should tolerate evil. Gandhi would nurse General Dyer if he were ill, but if his own son lived a life of shame, he would not help him by continuing to support him. On the contrary, "my love for him would require me to withdraw all support from him, although this might even mean his death." No one has the right to compel another by physical force to become good. "But one is under the obligation to resist him by leaving him, no matter what may happen, and by welcoming him to one's bosom if he repents."[2]

While Gandhi curbs the violent elements, he stimulates the hesitating. He reassures those who are afraid of taking a decisive step:

> Never has anything been done on this earth without direct action. I rejected the word "passive resistance" because of its insufficiency... It was, however, direct action in South Africa which told, and told so effectively that it converted General Smuts to sanity. What was the larger "symbiosis" that Buddha and Christ preached? Gentleness and love. Buddha fearlessly carried the war into the enemy's camp and brought down on its knees an arrogant priesthood. Christ drove out the money-changers from the temple of Jerusalem and drew down curses from heaven upon the hypocrites and the Pharisees. Both were for intensely direct action. But even as Buddha and Christ chastened,

---

1. At least so Gandhi interprets the texts. Dare a European venture that he finds in the Bhagavad Gitâ serene indifference to violence perpetrated and suffered?
2. August 25, 1920.

they showed unmistakable gentleness and love behind every act of theirs.[1]

Gandhi also appeals to the generosity and the common sense of the English.[2] He calls the English his "dear friends" and points out that he has been their faithful companion for more than thirty years. He asks them to make up for the Government's perfidy, which by its treachery has completely shattered his faith in its good intentions. But he still believes in English bravery and in English respect for other people's bravery. "Bravery on the battle-field is impossible for India, but bravery of the soul remains open to us. Non-coöperation means nothing less than training in self-sacrifice. I expect to conquer you by my suffering."

In the first four or five months' preliminary campaign Gandhi was not trying to paralyze the Government through non-coöperation; his idea was rather to lay the foundation for the building up of a new India which would be independent mentally, morally, and economically. Gandhi expresses the idea of India's economic independence by the term *Swadeshi*, and he takes the word in its narrow and physical sense.

India must learn to go without many comforts and to accept hardships without a murmur. A salutary discipline, this; necessary moral hygiene. The nation's health as well as its character will benefit thereby. Gandhi's first move is to free India from the curse of drink. Groups must be formed to advocate temperance. European wines must be boycotted; liquor-dealers must

1. May 12, 1920.
2. "To All the English in India," October 27, 1920.

be induced to surrender their licenses.[1] All India responded to the Mahatma's appeal. Such a strong wave of temperance swept over India that Gandhi had to interfere to prevent the crowds from sacking and looting the wine-shops and closing them by force. "You must not try to compel another by physical force to become good," he explained to the masses.

But if it was a relatively easy matter to rid India of the curse of drink, it was much more difficult to provide her with means of subsistence. If cooperation with England ceased, what would India live on? What would she clothe herself in if European products were tabooed? Gandhi's solution is one of utmost simplicity and reveals the medieval turn of his mind: he undertakes to reestablish the old Indian industry of home spinning, introduce the spinning-wheels.

This patriarchal solution of the social problem has naturally met with ridicule.[2] But conditions in India and Gandhi's interpretation of the term *charka* must, be taken into consideration. Gandhi has never claimed that spinning alone would constitute a means of livelihood except for the very poor; but he does claim that it could supplement agriculture during the months when work in the fields is at a standstill. India's problem is not theoretical, but real and pressing. Eighty per cent of the population

---

1. April 28, 1920; June 8, September 1, 1921. In his "Letter to the Parsees," the business people, he begs them to stop selling alcohol (March 23, 1921). In his "Letter to the Moderates," June 8, 1921, he asks them to help him carry this point, even if they do not agree with the other points of his program. He also wages war on drugs, narcotics, and opium dens.
2. Gandhi himself realizes that many will jeer. But, he asks, did the sewing-machine do away with the needle? The spinning-wheel's utility has not been lost. On the contrary, nothing is more useful at the present moment. Spinning is a national necessity, and constitutes the only possible means of subsistence for millions of starving people. (July 21, 1920.)

of India is agricultural, and is therefore without employment virtually four months of the year. One tenth of the population is normally exposed to famine. The middle class is underfed. What has England done to remedy these conditions? Nothing. On the contrary, she has aggravated them, for English manufactures have ruined local industries, pumped the resources of India, bleeding the country for more than sixty million rupees a year. India, who grows all the cotton she requires, is forced to export millions of bales to Japan and Lancashire, whence it is returned to her in the form of manufactured calico, which she must buy at exorbitant prices. The first thing for India to do, therefore, is to learn to do without ruinous foreign goods, and in order to do this she must organize workshops of her own to give employment and food to her people. There is no time to lose. Now, nothing can be organized more rapidly and economically than the industry of spinning and weaving at home. The idea is not to induce well paid agricultural laborers to give up their work and to spin, but to urge the unemployed, and all those who do not have to work for a living, such as women and children, as well as all Hindus who may have some spare time during the day, to spin in their leisure hours. Gandhi orders, therefore, (1) the boycotting of foreign goods, (2) the teaching of spinning and weaving, (3) the buying of hand-woven cloth only.

Gandhi gives himself up tirelessly to this idea. He says spinning is a duty for all India.[1] He wants poor children to pay for their tuition at school by a certain number of hours of spinning; he wants everyone, man and woman, to contribute at least one hour a day, as charity, to spinning. He gives the most precise directions as to the choice of cotton, spinning-wheels,

1. February 2, 1921.

etc., and information on all sorts of technical details of spinning and weaving; he gives practical advice to those who wish to buy hand-woven cloth, to the fathers of large families, as well as to pupils in the schools. He explains, for instance, how one may start a *Swadeshi* shop—a shop dealing in the products of Hindu industry—with but little capital, make ten per cent profits, etc. He becomes lyrical when he describes the "music of the spinning-wheel,"[1] the oldest music in India, which delighted Kahir, the poet-weaver, and Aureng-Zeb, the great emperor, who wove his own caps.

Gandhi was able to fire public enthusiasm. The great ladies of Bombay took up spinning. Hindu and Moslem women agreed to wear only national cloth, which became all the fashion. Tagore, too, praised this *khaddar* or *khadi*, as the hand-woven cloth was called, which he said was in excellent taste. Orders poured in. Some came from as far as Aden and Baluchistan.

But the disciples of *Swadeshi* went a little too far when they began boycotting foreign materials, and even Gandhi, usually sane and well balanced, was carried away. In August, 1921, he ordered the binning of all foreign goods in Bombay, and as in the days of Savonarola in Florence, *Christo regnante*, magnificent family heirlooms, priceless stuffs and materials, were piled into huge heaps and devoured by the flames in the midst of riotous cheers and enthusiasm. In this connection one of the most broad-minded Englishmen in India, C. F. Andrews, a great friend of Rabindranath Tagore, wrote a letter to Gandhi. While expressing his great admiration for the Mahatma, he deplored that such valuable materials should have been burned instead of having been given to the poor. He added that he believed

1. July 21, 1920.

the process of destruction called forth the worst instincts of the masses, and he protested against the outbursts of a nationalism which virtually set destruction up as a religious dogma. He could not help feeling that it was sinful to destroy the fruits of human toil. Andrews had approved Gandhi's campaign and had even begun wearing *khaddar* but now he wondered whether it was right to continue to do so. The burning cloth in Bombay had shaken his faith in the Mahatma.

In publishing Andrews's letter in "Young India" Gandhi said he regrets nothing. He does not bear ill will to any race whatsoever, nor does he demand the destruction of *all* foreign goods. He merely wants to destroy the goods which harm India. Millions of Indians have been ruined by English factories, which, by taking work away from India, have turned thousands upon thousands of Indians into pariahs and mercenaries and their women into prostitutes. India is already inclined to hate her British dominators. Gandhi does not wish to strengthen this hatred. On the contrary, he wants to side-track it, to turn it away from people to *things*. The Indians who bought the materials are as guilty as the British who sold them. The materials were not burned as an expression of hatred for England, but as a sign of India's determination to break with the past. It was a necessary surgical operation. And it would have been wrong to give these "poisonous" materials to the poor, for the poor too, have a sense of honor.

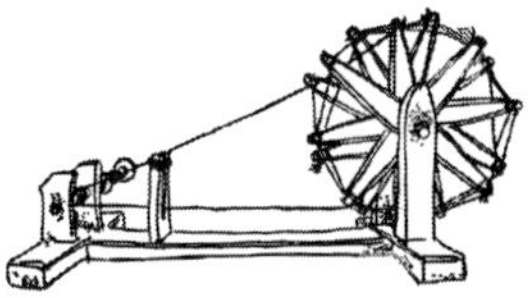

CHAPTER 3

India's economic life must first be freed from foreign domination. But the next step is to liberate the mind, create a real, independent Indian spirit. Gandhi wants his people to shake off the yoke of European culture, and one of his proudest achievements is the laying of the groundwork of a truly Indian education.

Under English rule the smoldering embers of Asiatic culture had lain dormant in various colleges and universities. For more than forty-five years Aligarh had remained a Hindu-Mussulman university, a center of Islamic culture in India. Khalsa College was the center of Sikh culture, while the Hindus had the University of Benares. But these institutions, more or less antiquated, were dependent on the Government, which subventioned them, and Gandhi longed to see them replaced by purer hearths of Asiatic culture. In November, 1920, he founded the national University of Gujarat at Ahmedabad. It's ideal was that of a united India. The *Dharma* of the Hindus and the Islam of the Mohammedans were its two religious pillars. Its object was to preserve the dialects of India and to use them as sources of national regeneration.[1] Gandhi felt, with full justice, that a "systematic study

1. November 17, 1920.

of Asiatic culture is no less essential than the study of Western sciences. The vast treasures of Sanskrit and Arabic, Persian and Pali and Magadhi, have to be ransacked to discover wherein lies the source of strength for the nation. The ideal is not merely to feed on or repeat the ancient cultures, but to build a new culture based on the traditions of the past and enriched by the experiences of later times. The ideal is a synthesis of the different cultures that have to come to stay in India, that have influenced Indian life, and that, in their turn, have themselves been influenced by the spirit of the soil. This synthesis will naturally be of the *Swadeshi* type, where each culture is assured its legitimate place, and not of the American pattern, where one dominant culture absorbs the rest and where the aim is not toward harmony, but toward an artificial and forced unity." All Indian religions were to be taught. The Hindus were to have an opportunity of studying the Koran and the Mussulmans the Shastras. The national university excludes nothing except a spirit of exclusion. It believes that there is nothing "untouchable" in humanity. Hindustani is made compulsory, because it is the national blend of Sanskrit, Hindi, and Persianized Urdu.[1] A spirit of independence was to be fostered, not only by the methods of study, but by a careful vocational training.

Gandhi hopes to organize, gradually, higher schools that will spread education broadcast throughout the towns and "filter it down to the masses, so that... ere long the suicidal cleavage between the educated and the uneducated will be bridged. And as an effect of giving an industrial education to the genteel folks

1. English is not excluded, nor any other European language, but it is reserved for the higher grades, at the end of the school program. In all grades, however, Indian dialects are used. Gandhi dreams of a higher state of universal existence where all differences will persist, not as divisions but as different facets.

and a literary education to the industrial classes, the unequal distribution of wealth and social discontent will be considerably checked."

In opposition to European educational methods, which neglect manual proficiency and develop the brain only, Gandhi wants manual work to be part of the curriculum of all the schools from the lowest grades up. He believes it would be excellent for children to pay for their tuition by a certain amount of spinning. In this way they would learn to earn their living and become independent. As for education of the heart, which Europe neglects absolutely, Gandhi would have stress laid upon it from the very first. But before the pupils can be properly trained, the right sort of teachers must be provided.

The object of the higher institutions which Gandhi seems to look upon as the keystones of the new education is to train teachers. These institutions will be more than schools or colleges; they might rather be called convents, where the sacred fire of India will be concentrated in order afterward to radiate throughout the world, just as in former days great religious pioneers radiated from the Benedictine monasteries in the West, conquering souls and territory.

The rules which Gandhi prescribes for the school of *Satyagrah Ashram*,[1] or place of discipline, at Ahmedabad, his model institution, concern the teachers more than the pupils, and bind the former by monastic vows. Whereas these vows in ordinary religious orders have a purely negative character, here they throb with an active spirit of sacrifice and with the pure love that inspires the saints. The teachers are bound by the following vows:

1. *Ashram*, place of discipline, hermitage.

1. The vow of truth. It is not enough not to resort ordinarily to untruth. No deception may be practiced even for the good of the country. Truth may require opposition to parents and elders.

2. The vow of *Ahimsa* (non-killing). It is not enough not to take the life of any living being. One may not even hurt those whom he believes to be unjust; he may not be angry with them, he must love them. Oppose tyranny but never hurt the tyrant. Conquer him by love. Suffer punishment even unto death for disobeying his will.

3. The vow of celibacy. Without it the two foregoing are almost impossible to observe. It is not enough not to look upon woman with a lustful eye. Animal passions must be controlled, so that they will not be moved even in thought. If a man is married, he will consider his wife a lifelong friend and establish with her the relationship of perfect purity.

4. The control of the palate. Regulate and purify the diet. Leave off such foods as may tend to stimulate animal passions or are otherwise unnecessary.

5. The vow of non-stealing. It is not enough not to steal what is commonly considered other men's property. It is theft if we use articles which we do not really need. Nature provides us from day to day just enough and no more for our daily needs.

6. The vow of non-possession. It is not enough not to possess and not to keep much, but it is necessary not to keep anything which may not be absolutely necessary for our bodily wants. Think constantly of simplifying life.

To these main vows are added a few secondary rules:

1. *Swadeshi.* Use no articles about which there is a possibility of deception. Do not use manufactured articles. Laborers suffer much in mills, and manufactured articles are products of

misery exploited. Foreign goods and goods made by complicated machinery should be tabooed by a votary of *Ahimsa.* Use simple clothes, made simply in India.

2. Fearlessness. He who is acted upon by fear cannot follow truth or *Ahimsa.* He must be free from the fear of kings, people, caste, families, thieves, robbers, ferocious animals, and death. A truly fearless man will defend himself against others by truth-force or soul-force.

Once established the main points of this iron foundation, Gandhi refers rapidly to the other requirements, of which the two most remarkable are that the teachers must set the example of performing bodily labor, preferably agricultural work, and that they must know the principal Indian tongues.

As for the pupils, who can enter the *Ashram* from the age of four up (students will be admitted at any age), they must remain in the *Ashram* for the whole course of studies, which lasts about ten years. The children are separated from their parents and families. The parents renounce all authority over them. The children never visit their parents. The pupils wear simple clothes, eat simple food of a strictly vegetarian nature, have no holidays in the ordinary sense of the word, though once a week they are allowed a day and a half in which to do individual creative work. Three months of the year are spent in traveling on foot through India. All pupils must study the Hindi and Dravidian dialects. As a second language, they must learn English, and they must also familiarize themselves with the characters of the five Indian languages (Urdu, Bengali, Tamil, Telugu, and Davanagri). They are taught, in their own dialect, history, geography, mathematics, economics, and Sanskrit. At the same time they are taught agriculture and spinning and weaving. It goes without saying that a religious atmosphere pervades the whole education.

When they have completed their studies, the pupils are allowed to choose between taking the vows, like their teachers, or leaving the school. The tuition is entirely free.

I have described Gandhi's educational system rather fully because it shows the high spirituality of his action, and because he considers this system the mainspring of the whole movement. To build a New India, a new soul, strong and pure, must be wrought out of Indian elements. And this soul can only be developed by a sacred legion of apostles who, like those of Christ, will be as the salt of the earth. Gandhi, unlike our European revolutionaries, is not a maker of laws and ordinances. He is a builder of a new humanity.

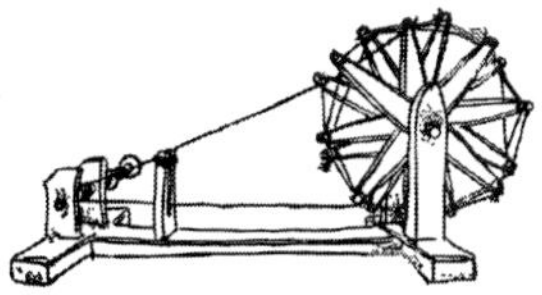

CHAPTER 4

Like all governments under similar conditions, the English Government had no realization of what was going on. At first its attitude was one of ironical disdain. The viceroy, Lord Chelmsford, characterized the movement in August, 1920, as "the most foolish of all foolish schemes." But these heights of comfortable condescension had to be abandoned before long. In November, 1920, the Government published a surprised and slightly alarmed proclamation, where threats and paternal advice commingled, warning the people that while the leaders of the movement had not been molested so far because they had not preached violence, orders had now been given to arrest anyone who overstepped the bounds and whose words might stir up revolt or in other ways incite to violence.

The bounds were soon overstepped, but by the Government. The non-coöperation movement had been growing and gathering momentum, and the Government was beginning to be seriously alarmed. In December affairs took a decidedly dangerous turn. Until then non-violent non-coöperation had been looked upon as an experiment of a more or less temporary nature, and the Government had flattered itself that when the National Indian Congress met at Nagpur for its December session, non-coöperation would be vetoed. But far from disapproving of non-coöperation, the congress incorporated the idea in the constitution by making the first paragraph read:

> The object of the Indian National Congress is the attainment of *Swaraj*—Home Rule—by the people of India by all legitimate and peaceful means.

The congress thereupon confirmed the non-coöperation resolution passed in the special session in September, and enlarged upon it. While the principle of non-violence was upheld absolutely, the general feeling was that every effort must be made to unite all the elements in India in view of a common, sustained action, and the congress not only called upon Hindus and Mussulmans to collaborate loyally, but urged a *rapprochement* between the privileged and "suppressed" classes. In addition to this the congress made fundamental changes in the constitution, which virtually amounted to the organization of a representative system for all India.[1]

---

1. At the Nagpur session of the congress some 4726 delegates were present, and among them were 469 Mohammedans, 65 Sikhs, 5 Parsees, 2 Untouchables, 4079 Hindus and 106 women.

   The new constitution provided that a delegate should be chosen for every 5000 inhabitants, which would make a total of 6175 delegates. The National Indian Congress was to meet once a year, round Christmas. The committee of the congress consisting of 850 members would act as executive body, enforcing the resolutions of the congress and carrying out its policies. Between the sessions of the congress the committee was to have the same authority as the congress. Within the committee an executive board of fifteen members was to bear the same relation to the congress committee that a ministerial cabinet bears to parliament. This board could be dissolved by the congress committee.

   The Congress of Nagpur drew up the plans for a hierarchy of committees of provincial congresses, representing twenty-one provinces and twelve

The congress did not try to conceal the fact that it regarded non-coöperation in its present form as a preliminary step only, to be followed, at a time to be determined later, by complete non-coöperation, including a refusal to pay taxes. Until then, however, and in order to pave the way, it urged that the boycott be sharpened, spinning and weaving be encouraged, while an appeal was sent out to students, parents, and magistrates inviting them to practice non-coöperation with greater zeal. Those who did not live up to the decisions of the congress were to be barred from public life.

The resolutions of the congress implied the virtual establishment of a state within a state, the setting up of real Indian rule in opposition to the British Government. England could not countenance this. She had to do something. The Government had to fight or negotiate. A compromise could easily have been reached by negotiation if the Government had been willing to go half-way. The congress had declared that it hoped to reach its goal "with England, if possible," but otherwise "without her." But as is always the case when European politics involve foreign races, no attempt was made to negotiate. Force was resorted to. Pretexts for armed oppression were sought. There was no lack of them.

Despite the principle of non-violence established by Gandhi and the congress, a few riots occurred in various parts of India.

---

languages, and placed under them local committees in each village or group of villages. It advised the formation of a band of national workers to be called the Indian National Service to be financed out of funds called the All-India Tilak Memorial Swaraja Fund.

Every adult, male or female, possessing 4 annas was given the right to vote, provided he had signed the credo of the constitution. Whoever has attained the age of twenty-one and has sworn adherence to Article I of the Constitution and agreed to uphold the rules and by-laws of the constitution is eligible.

It is true that they bore little or no relation to the non-coöperative movement, but, still, there had been and were troubles. In the United Provinces (Allahabad) there were agrarian uprisings, revolts of the tenants against the landowners, and the police had to interfere, and there was some bloodshed. Soon afterward the Akali movement of the Sikhs, although of a purely religious character, adopted non-coöperative methods, and as a result of the agitation some two hundred Sikhs were massacred in February, 1921. No one in good faith could have held Gandhi or his disciples responsible for this drama of fanaticism, but the Government considered it a good opportunity. In March, 1921, the repression began, and it became more and more oppressive as the months passed. The Government justified its intervention by the necessity of protecting the liquor dealers from the fury of the mobs. This was not the first time for European civilization and alcohol to march hand in hand. The volunteer non-coöperation organizations were dissolved. A law was made prohibiting seditious meetings. In certain provinces the police had given *carte blanche* in suppressing the movement, which was called "revolutionary and anarchistic." Thousands of Indians were arrested, and some of India's most respected citizens were summarily jailed and brutalized. Naturally, this procedure stirred up bad blood, and here and there the people and the constables clashed. Some houses were burned and people pounded. This was the situation in India when the committee of the All-Indian congress met at Bezwada in the end of March to discuss civil disobedience. With rare moderation and foresight it voted against it, on the ground that the country was not yet prepared to wield this double-edged sword. Civil disobedience would be urged later. For the present there could only be a sort of civil and financial mobilization.

Meanwhile Gandhi continued more and more actively his campaign for the unity of India. He tried to unite all religions, races, parties, and castes. He called upon the Parsees,[1] the rich, prosperous merchant class, more or less tainted, as he expressed it, with the spirit of Rockefeller, and he called upon Hindus and Mussulmans to form a solid alliance. The relations between Hindus and Mussulmans were continually embittered by prejudices, mutual fear, and suspicion. Gandhi devoted himself to bringing the two races into harmonious collaboration,[2] and without advocating or desiring an impossible fusion between the two peoples, he tried to unite them in friendship.[3]

His keenest efforts, however, were given to the regeneration of the "suppressed" classes, the pariahs. His passionate appeals for the pariahs, his cries of sorrow and indignation at the monstrous social iniquity which oppressed them, would, alone, immortalize his name. His feeling for the outcasts dates back to his boyhood. He tells how, when he was a boy,[4] a pariah used to come to the house

1. March 23, 1921.
2. October 6, 1920; May 11 and 18, July 28, October 20, 1921.
3. In citing his friendship with the Mussulman Maulana Mohamed Ali, Gandhi claims that both men remain true to their respective faiths.

   Gandhi would not give his daughter in marriage to one of Ali's sons, nor would he share the meals of his friend; and the same is true of Maulana Mohamed Ali. But this does not prevent both men from being fond of each other, respecting each other, and relying on each other.

   Gandhi does not say that intermarriage between Hindus and Mussulmans, and the fact of eating together, should necessarily be condemned, but he says they are impossible at the present time. It will take at least a century for the two peoples to reach such a stage of fusion. A policy purported practical should not attempt to carry such a reform. Gandhi does not object to it but considers it premature. The only important thing, for the present, is for the two peoples to respect each other and remain loyal to each other. Here, too, Gandhi shows his sense of realities. (October 20, 1921.)
4. Speech made April 27, 1921.

to do all the course work. As a boy Gandhi was told never to touch the pariah without purifying himself afterward by ablutions. He could not understand why, and often asked his parents about it. At school he frequently touched the untouchables, and his mother told him that he could escape the consequences of this unholy touch only by touching a Mohammedan. To Gandhi it all seemed absurdly unfair, cruelly unjustified. At the age of twelve he made up his mind to wipe this stain off India's conscience. He planned to come to the rescue of his degraded brothers. And never has Gandhi's mind revealed itself clearer and more unbiased than when he pleads their cause. What their cause means to him may be gathered from the fact that he says he would give up his religion (he to whom religion is everything!) if anyone can prove to him that untouchability is one of its dogmas. The unjust pariah system justified, in his eyes, everything that has been inflicted on India by other nations.

> If the Indians have become the pariahs of the empire, it is retributive justice, meted out to us by a just God... Should we Hindus not wash our blood-stained hands before we ask the English to wash theirs? Untouchability has degraded us, made us pariahs in South Africa, East Africa, Canada. So long as Hindus willfully regard untouchability as part of their religion, so long *Swaraj* is impossible of attainment. India is guilty, England has done nothing blacker. The first duty is to protect the weak and helpless and never injure the feelings of any individual. We are no better than brutes until we have purged ourselves of the sins we have committed against our weaker brethren.

Gandhi wanted the national congress to better the condition of the pariah brothers by giving them schools and wells, for pariahs were not allowed to use the public wells. But until then? Unable to wait with folded hands for the privileged classes to condescend to make good their cruelty, Gandhi went over to the pariahs. He placed himself at their head and tried to organize them. He discussed their problems with them. What ought they to do? Appeal to the English Government? Place themselves at its disposal? This would only mean a change of slavery. Abandon Hinduism? (Note the broad-minded audacity of a Hindu believer!) Become Christians or Mohammedans? Gandhi would almost advise them to do so if Hinduism really stood for untouchability. But it doesn't. Untouchability is only a morbid excrescence of Hinduism, which must be extirpated. The pariahs must organize themselves in self-defense. They might, of course, adopt the principles of non-coöperation in regard to Hinduism by refusing to have any relations with the Hindus (singularly audacious advice of social revolt on the lips of a patriot like Gandhi!). But the difficulty is that the pariahs have no leaders and cannot organize themselves. The best thing, therefore, is for them to join the general non-coöperation movement, since its object is harmony among all classes. Real non-coöperation is a religious act of purification, and no one can take part in it who believes in untouchability. Gandhi in this way combines religion, humanity, and patriotism.[1]

A certain solemnity attended the first efforts to group the pariahs. A "suppressed-classes conference" took place at Ahmedabad on April 13 and 14, 1921. Gandhi presided at the conference and made one of his most beautiful speeches. He not only demanded the suppression of the pariah system but urged the untouchables to rise to the occasion and show the best that was in them.

---

1. October 27, 1920.

He expects great things from the pariahs, he says, in the social life of regenerated India. He tries to instill self-confidence in them and fill them with his own burning ideal. In the "suppressed classes," he says, he sees tremendous latent possibilities. He believes that within five months the untouchable class will be able to win, by its own merits, the place it deserves within the great Indian family.

Gandhi had the joy of seeing his appeal find echo in the hearts of the people. In many parts of India the pariahs were emancipated.[1] The day before his arrest Gandhi made a speech recording the progress of the pariah cause. The Brahmans were helping. The privileged classes were giving touching examples of remorse and fraternal love. Gandhi cites the case of a young Brahman who at nineteen became a street-sweeper, to live among the untouchables.[2]

1. In the end of April, 1921, untouchability begins to diminish. In many villages the pariahs are allowed to live among other Hindus and to enjoy the same rights. (April 27, 1921.) In other regions, however, their condition remains deplorable, particularly in Madras. (September 29, 1921.) The question is included in the program of the National Assemblies of India from this time on. The Congress of Nagpur, in December, 1920, had already expressed the desire of seeing untouchability wiped out.
2. April 27, 1921.

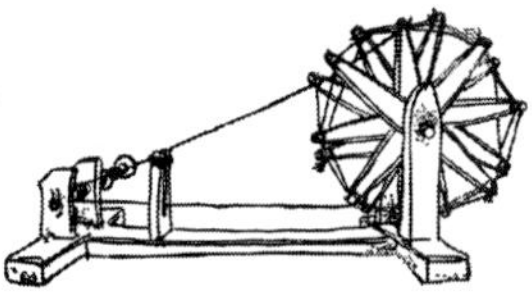

CHAPTER 5

With equal generosity Gandhi took up another great cause, that of women.

The sexual problem is a peculiarly difficult one in India, throbbing with an all-pervading, oppressive, and badly directed sensuality. Child marriages weaken the physical and moral resources of the nation. The obsession of the flesh weighs on men's minds and is an insult to woman's dignity. Gandhi publishes the complaints of Hindu women at the degrading attitude of Hindu nationalists.[1] Gandhi takes the women's side. Their protest, he says, proves that there is another sore in India as bad as that of untouchability. But the woman question is not a purely Indian problem. The whole world suffers from it. As with the pariahs, he expects more from the oppressed than from the oppressors. He calls upon women to demand and inspire respect by ceasing to think of themselves as the objects of masculine desire only. Let them forget their bodies and enter into public life, assume the risks, and suffer the consequences of their convictions. Women should not only renounce luxury and throw away or burn foreign goods, but they should share men's problems and privations.

1. July 21, 1921, and October 6, 1920.

Many distinguished women have faced arrest and imprisonment in Calcutta. This shows the proper spirit. Instead of asking for mercy, women should vie with men in suffering for the cause. When it comes to suffering, women will always surpass men. Let women have no fear. The weakest will be able to preserve her honor. "One who knows how to die need never fear."

Nor does Gandhi forget the fallen sisters.[1] He tells of conversations with them in the provinces of Andhra and Barisal, where they met in conference. He spoke to them nobly and simply, and they replied, confided in him, and asked his advice. He tried to suggest some way in which they might make an honest living, and proposed spinning. They agreed to begin the very next day if assured of encouragement and assistance. And then Gandhi turned to the men of India; called upon them to respect women:

> Gambling in vice has no place in our revolution. *Swaraj*, home rule, means that we must regard every inhabitant of India as our own brother or sister. Woman is not the weaker sex, but the better half of humanity, the nobler of the two; for even to-day it is the embodiment of sacrifice, silent suffering, humility, faith, and knowledge. Woman's intuition has often proved truer than man's arrogant assumption of knowledge.

In the women of India, beginning with his own wife, Gandhi always found intelligent aid and understanding, and among them he recruited some of his best disciples.

1. July 21, August 11, December 16, 1921.

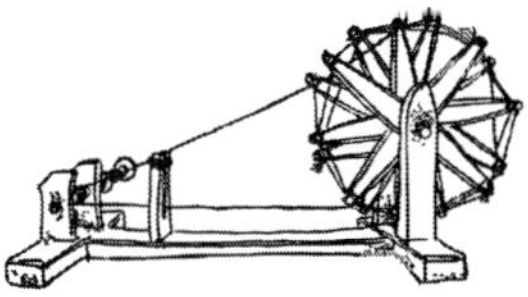

CHAPTER 6

In 1921 Gandhi's power was at its apogee. His authority as a moral leader was vast, and without having sought it, almost limited political authority had been placed in his hand. The people looked upon him as a saint. Pictures were painted representing him as Sri-Krishna.[1] And at the end of the year, in December, the All-India National Congress delegated its powers to him and authorized him to appoint his successor. He was the undisputed master of India's policy. It was up to him to start a political revolution, if he saw fit, or even to reform religion.

He did not do so. He did not wish to do so. Moral grandeur? Moral hesitancy? Both, perhaps. It is very difficult for one human being really to understand another, particularly if they belong to different races and civilizations. And how much more difficult when a spirit so deep and subtle as Gandhi's is to be considered! In the maze of events which took place in India, in this tumultuous year, it is hard to ascertain whether the pilot's hand did not tremble, but, always firm and sure, steered the colossal ship along the chosen course. I will try, however, to explain my feeling in regard to the living enigma, and I will do so with the religious

1. Gandhi protests against this in "Young India" of June, 1921.

respect which I have for this great man and the sincerity which I owe to his sincerity.

If Gandhi's power was great, the danger of abusing it was equally great. As the effect of his campaign, by the slightest ripple, affected hundreds of millions of men, it became more and more difficult to direct the movement and at the same time remain firm in the midst of the turbulent ocean. A superhuman problem indeed, to conciliate moderation and high-mindedness with surging, unbridled mob passions! The pilot, gentle and pious, prays and relies on God; but the voice that comes to him is almost lost in the roar of the tempest. Will it ever reach the others?

There is no danger of his being swept off his feet by pride. No amount of adoration can turn his head. On the contrary, it wounds not only his sense of fitness of things, but his spirit of humility. Gandhi is an exception among prophets and mystics, for he sees no visions, has no revelations; he does not try to persuade himself that he is guided supernaturally, nor does he try to make others believe it. Radiant sincerity is his. His forehead remains calm and clear, his heart devoid of vanity. He is a man, like all other men. He is *not* a saint. He will not have the people call him one. (Yet his very attitude proves that he is one.)

The word "saint," he says, should be ruled out of present life.

> I pray like every good Hindu. I believe we can all be messengers of God. I have no special revelations of God's will. My firm belief is that He reveals himself daily to every human being, but that we shut our cars to the "still small voice."... I claim to be nothing but a humble servant of India and humanity. I have no desire to found a sect. I am really too ambitious to be satisfied with a sect for

a following, for I represent no new truths. I endeavor to follow and represent truth as I know it. I do claim to throw a new light on many an old truth.[1]

Personally, he is always modest, conscientious in the extreme, incapable of narrow-mindedness whether as Indian patriot or apostle of non-coöperation. He sanctions no tyranny, not even for the good of the cause. Government oppression must never be replaced by non-coöperative oppression.[2] Gandhi will not set his country up against other countries; his patriotism is not confined to the boundaries of India. "For me, patriotism is the same as humanity. I am patriotic because I am human and humane. My patriotism is not exclusive. I will not hurt England or Germany to serve India. Imperialism has no place in my scheme of life. A patriot is so much less a patriot if he is a lukewarm humanitarian."[3]

But have his disciples always felt this way? And, on their lips, what becomes of Gandhi's doctrine? And, interpreted by them, how does it reach the masses?

When Rabindranath Tagore, after traveling several years in Europe, returned to India in August, 1921, he was astounded at the change in the mentality of the people. Even before his return he had expressed his anxiety in a series of letters sent from Europe to friends in India. Many of these letters were published in his "Modern Review."[4] The controversy between Tagore and Gandhi,

---

1. May 12, 1920; May 25, July 13, August 25, 1921.
2. December 8, 1920.
3. March 16, 1921.
4. "Letters from Abroad." The three letters of March 2, 5, and 13 were published in the "Modern Review" in May, 1921. The "Appeal to Truth" was written after Tagore's return to India and published in the "Modern Review" October 1, 1921. The two men, however, did not discuss their views in polemical writings only. They met and had a long interview, but neither has published any

between two great minds, both moved by mutual admiration and esteem, but as fatally separated in their feeling as a philosopher can be from an apostle, a St. Paul from a Plato, is important. For on the one side we have the spirit of religious faith and charity seeking to found a new humanity. On the other we have intelligence, free-born, serene, and broad, seeking to unite aspirations of all humanity in sympathy and understanding.

Tagore always looked upon Gandhi as a saint, and I have often heard him speak of him with veneration. When, in referring to the Mahatma, I mentioned Tolstoi, Tagore pointed out to me, and I realize it now that I know Gandhi better—how much more clothed in light and radiance Gandhi's spirit is than Tolstoi's. With Gandhi everything is nature—modest, simple, pure—while all his struggles are hallowed by religious serenity, whereas with Tolstoi everything is proud revolt against pride, hatred against hatred, passion against passion. Everything in Tolstoi is violence, even his doctrine of non-violence. On April 10, 1921, Tagore wrote from London, "We are grateful to Gandhi for giving India a chance to prove that her faith in the divine spirit of man is still living." Despite the misgivings he had expressed as to Gandhi's campaign, Tagore, when he left France to return to India, sincerely planned to back Gandhi in every way. And even the manifesto of October, 1921, which I will discuss later—the "Appeal to Truth," which marked the break between the two men—begins with one of the most beautiful tributes to Gandhi that have ever been written.

Gandhi's attitude to Tagore is one of loving regard, and it does not change even when the two disagree. You feel that Gandhi

---

comment on their meeting. C. F. Andrews, however, who was present, has told us what the talk was about and referred to the arguments used by Tagore and Gandhi to back up their different points of view.

is loath to enter into polemics with Tagore, and when certain kind friends try to embitter the debate by repeating personal remarks, Gandhi bids them be silent and explains how much he owes Tagore.[1]

Yet it was inevitable that the breach between the two men would widen. As far back as in 1920 Tagore had deplored that the overflowing wealth of Gandhi's love and faith should be made to serve political ends, as it had since Tilak's death. Of course Gandhi had not entered the political arena with a light heart. But when Tilak died, India was left without a political leader, and someone had to take his place.

As Gandhi says:[2]

> If I seem to take part in politics, it is only because politics to-day encircle us like the coils of a snake from which one cannot get out no matter how one tries. I wish to wrestle with the snake... I am trying to introduce religion into politics.

But this Tagore deplores. Writing September 7, 1920, he says, "We need all the moral force which Mahatma Gandhi represents, and which he alone in the world can represent." That such a precious treasure should be cast out on the frail bark of politics and subjected to the incessant lashing of the waves of conflicting and irritated passions is a serious misfortune for India, whose mission, says Tagore, "is to awaken the dead to life by soul-fire." The wasting of spiritual resources in problems which,

1. February 9, 1922. In this article, called "Too Sacred for Publication," Gandhi dwells on his long friendship with Tagore. Gandhi was a frequent visitor at Tagore's home at Santiniketan, and considered it as a retreat. While he was in England his children had their home there.
2. May 12, 1920.

when considered in the light of abstract moral truth, are unworthy, is to be regretted. "It is criminal to transform moral force into force."

This is what Tagore felt at the spectacular launching of the non-coöperation campaign and at the unrest stirred up in the name of the Khilafat cause and the massacres of the Punjab. He feared the results of the campaign on an easily excitable mob subject to attacks of hysterical fury. He would have liked to turn people's minds away from vengeance and dreams of impossible redress; he would have had them forget the irreparable and devote all efforts to constructing and fashioning a new soul for India. And although he admired Gandhi's doctrines and the ardent fire of his spirit of self-sacrifice, he hated the element of negation contained in non-coöperation. Tagore instinctively recoiled from everything that stood for "No."

And this conviction leads him to compare the positive ideal of Brahmanism, which demands that the joys of life be welcomed but purified, to the negative ideal of Buddhism, which demands their suppression.[1] To this Gandhi replies that the art of eliminating is as vital as that of accepting.[2] Human progress consists in a combination of the two. The final word in the Upanishads is a negation. The definition of Brahman by the authors of the Upanishads is *neti*, not this! India had lost the power of saying "No." Gandhi has given it back to her. Weeding is as essential as sowing.

But Tagore, apparently, does not believe in weeding. In his poetic contemplation of life he is satisfied with things as they are, and he finds his delight in admiring their harmony. He explains

1. March 5, 1921.
2. June 1, 1921.

his point of view in lines of great beauty, but detached from real life. His words are like the dance of Nataraja, a play of illusions. Tagore says he tries to tune his spirit up to the great exaltation that is sweeping over the country. But he cannot do so, for in his heart, despite himself, is a spirit of resistance. "In the darkness of my despair," he says, "I see a smile and hear a voice that says, 'Your place is with the children, playing on the beaches of the world, and there I am with you.'" Tagore plays with harmonies, invents new rhythms, "strung out through the hours, like children dancing in the sun and laughing as they disappear." All creation is happy, with Tagore; flowers and leaves are merely rhythms that never cease. God Himself is the supreme juggler, who plays with Time, tossing stars and planets out upon the torrent of appearances, and dropping paper boats filled with dreams into the river of the ages. "When I beg Him to let me be His disciple and to let me place some of the toys of my invention into one of his merry barks. He smiles, and I follow Him, clutching the hem of his gown." Here Tagore feels he is in his place. "But where am I, in a great crowd, squeezed in at all sides? And who can understand the noise I hear? If I hear a song, my sitar can catch the melody, and I can join the chorus, for I am a singer. But in the mad clamor of the crowd, my voice is lost, and I become dizzy." Tagore has tried, in the clamor of non-coöperation, to find a melody, but to no avail. And he says to himself: "If you can't march in step with your compatriots in the greatest crisis of their history, beware of saying they are in the wrong, and you in the right! But give up your place in the ranks, go back to your poet's corner, and be prepared to meet with ridicule and public disgrace."[1]

---

1. March 5, 1921.

So would a Goethe speak, an Indian Goethe, Bacchus. And it would seem as if Tagore's mind is made up from now on. The poet bids action farewell, since this action implies a negation, and he withdraws back into the spell of creative enchantment he weaves around himself. But Tagore does not only withdraw. As he says, Fate had decided that he should steer his bark against the current. At the time he was not only the "poet" but the spiritual ambassador of Asia to Europe; he had just returned from Europe, where he had asked people to coöperate in creating a world university at Santiniketan. What an irony of destiny that he should be preaching cooperation between Occident and Orient at one end of the world, when at that very moment non-coöperation was being preached at the other end![1]

Non-coöperation wounded him doubly, therefore, in his work as well as in his conception of life. "I believe," he says, "in the real union of Orient and Occident."

Non-coöperation clashed with his way of thinking, for his mentality, his rich intelligence, had been nourished on all the cultures of the world. "All humanity's greatest is mine," he says. "The *infinite personality of man* (as the Upanishads say) can only come from the magnificent harmony of all human races. My prayer is that India may represent the coöperation of all the peoples of the world. For India, unity is truth, and division evil. Unity is that which embraces and understands everything; consequently, it cannot be attained through negation. The present attempt to separate our spirit from that of the Occident is an attempt at spiritual suicide... The present age has been dominated by the Occident, because the Occident had a mission to fulfill. We of the Orient should learn from the Occident. It is regrettable,

1. March 6, 1921.

of course, that we had lost the power of appreciating our own culture, and therefore did not know how to assign Western culture to its right place. But to say that it is wrong to coöperate with the West is to encourage the worst form of provincialism and can produce nothing but intellectual indigence. The problem is a world problem. No nation can find its own salvation by breaking away from others. We must all be saved or we must all perish together."[1]

In other words, just as Goethe in 1818 refused to reject French civilization and culture, Tagore refuses to banish Western civilization. While Gandhi's doctrine does not really set a barrier up between the East and West, Tagore knows it will be interpreted as doing so, once Hindu nationalism is stirred. Tagore fears the development of the spirit of exclusion, and he explains his feeling of doubt and anxiety when his students at the beginning of the non-cooperation movement came to seek his advice. What does the boycotting of schools and colleges mean? asks Tagore. "That students shall make a sacrifice—for what? Not for a more complete education, but for non-education." During the first *Swadeshi* campaign[2] a group of young students told him that they would leave their schools and colleges at once if he ordered them to do so. And when he refused to do so, they left him, in much irritation, doubting his patriotism.[3]

In the spring of 1921, when India began boycotting English schools, Tagore had seen an aggressive example of intellectual nationalism in London. During a lecture of one of Tagore's friends. Professor Pearson, some Indian students gave vent to misplaced

1. March 13, 1921. Developed in article in the "Modern Review" of November, 1921.
2. The first Indian home rule campaign, in Bengal, in 1907-08.
3. March 5, 1921.

national manifestations. Tagore became indignant, and in a letter addressed to the director of Santiniketan he condemned this spirit of intolerance and held the non-coöperation movement responsible for it. And to this accusation Gandhi replies:

> I do not want my house to be walled in on all sides and my windows to be stuffed. I want the culture of all lands to be blown about my house as freely as possible... But I refuse to be blown off my feet by any of them... Mine is not a religion of the prison-house. It has room for the least among God's creations. But it is proof against insolent pride of race, religion, or color.

While expressing his doubts as to the merits of an English literary education, which has nothing to do with the building up of character, an education which, he said, has emasculated the youth of India, Gandhi regretted the excesses mentioned and claimed that his attitude was not narrow, as Tagore seemed to imply.

These were frank and noble words, but they did not disarm Tagore's misgivings. Tagore did not doubt Gandhi, but he feared the Gandhists. And from the first contact with his people, after his return from Europe, he began to fear the blind faith which the people placed in the Mahatma's words. Tagore saw the danger of mental despotism loom near, and in the "Modern Review" of October, 1921, he published a real manifesto, "An Appeal to Truth," which was a cry of revolt against this blind obedience. The protest was particularly strong because it was preceded by a beautiful homage to the Mahatma. After describing the first Indian independence movement in 1907 and 1908, Tagore explained that in those days the political leaders were inspired by a bookish ideal, based on the traditions of Burke, Gladstone,

Mazzini, and Garibaldi, and their message could be understood only by the elite. They advanced, in short, an English-speaking ideal. But then came Mahatma Gandhi! He stopped at the thresholds of the thousands of disinherited, dressed like one of their own. He spoke to them in their own language. Here was truth at last, and not only quotations from books! Mahatma, the name given by the people of India to Gandhi, is his real name. For who else had felt, like him, in communion with the people? Felt that they are of his own flesh and blood? At the Mahatma's call the hidden forces of the soul have blossomed forth, for the Mahatma has made the truth into something concrete, visible. In the same way, thousands of years ago, India blossomed forth to new greatness at Buddha's call, when he made men understand that there must be compassion and fellow-feeling among all living creatures. India, stirred to new life, expressed her strength in science and wealth, spreading across oceans and deserts. No commercial or military conquests ever spread so magnificently. For love alone is truth.

But then Tagore's tone changed. The apotheosis stopped. Deception followed. In Europe, across the seas, Tagore felt the quiver of India's great revival. Thrilled, filled with joy at the thought of breathing in the fluid breeze of the new freedom, he returned to his home land. But on his arrival his elation fell. An oppressive atmosphere weighed on the people. "An outside influence seemed to be bearing down on them, grinding them and making one and all speak in the same tone, follow in the same groove. Everywhere I was told that culture and reasoning power should abdicate, and blind obedience only reign. So simple it is to crush, in the name of some outward liberty, the real freedom of the soul!"

We understand Tagore's misgivings and his appeal. They are of all times and ages. The last free minds of a crumbling old world voiced them at the dawn of the new Christianity. And whenever we ourselves encounter the rising tide of some blind faith in a social or national ideal we feel the same misgivings stir within us. Tagore's revolt is the revolt of the free soul against the ages of faith which it has suscitated, for while faith to a handful of chosen ones means supreme liberty, it means only another form of slavery for the masses who are led by it.

Tagore's criticism is aimed above and beyond the fanaticism of the crowd. Over the blind masses it strikes the Mahatma. No matter how great Gandhi may be, isn't he taking upon himself more than a single man can bear? A cause as great as India's should not be dependent on the will of a single master. The Mahatma is the master of truth and love, but the attainment of *Swaraj* home rule, is vastly complicated. "The paths are intricate and hard to explore. Emotion and enthusiasm are required, but also science and meditation. All the moral forces of the nation must be called upon. Economists must find practical solutions, educators must teach, statesmen ponder, workers work... Everywhere the desire to learn must be kept up free and unhampered. No pressure, either open or hidden, must weigh on the intelligence."... "In older days, in our primeval forests," says Tagore, "our sages, *gurus*, in the plenitude of their vision, called on *all* seekers of truth... Why does not our *guru*, who wants to lead us to action, make the same call?" But the only command that *Guru Gandhi* so far has launched is, "Spin and weave!" And Tagore asks, "Is this the gospel of a new creative age? If large machinery constitutes a danger for the West, will not small machines constitute a greater danger for us?" The forces of a nation must cooperate, not only with each other, but with other nations. "The awakening of

India is bound up in the awakening of the world. Every nation that tries to shut itself in violates the spirit of the new age." And Tagore, who has spent several years in Europe, speaks of some of the men he met—men who have freed their hearts from the chains of nationalism in order to serve humanity—men who constitute the persecuted minority of world citizens, *cives totius orbis*—and he classes them among the *sannyasins*, that is, "those who in their soul have realized human unity."[1]

And should India alone, asks Tagore, recite the chapter of negation, dwell eternally on the faults of others, and strive for *Swaraj* on a basis of hatred? When the bird is awakened by the dawn, it does not only think of food. Its wings respond to the call of the sky. Its throat fills with joyous songs to greet the coming day. A new humanity has sent out its call. Let India reply in her own way! "Our first duty, at dawn, is to remember *Him Who is One, who is indistinguishable through class or color, and who, by his varied forces, provides, as is necessary, for the needs of each class and of all. Let us pray Him, who gives wisdom, to unite us all in understanding.*"[2]

Tagore's noble words, some of the most beautiful ever addressed to a nation, are a poem of sunlight, and plane above all human struggles. And the only criticism one can make of them is that they plane too high. Tagore is right, from the point of view of eternity. The bird-poet, the eagle-sized lark, as Heine called a master of our music, sits and sings on the ruins of time. He lives in eternity. But the demands of the present are imperious. The hour that passes demands immediate, if imperfect, relief; but clamors for it. And in this respect Gandhi, who lacks

1. Those who have renounced their personal life in order to bring a unity to mankind.
2. Paraphrase of the first stanza of the Upanishads.

Tagore's poetic flight (or who, perhaps, as a *Boddhisattva* of pity has given it up in order to live among the disinherited) finds it child's play to reply.

In his answer to Tagore Gandhi displays more passion than he has so far shown in the controversy. On October 13, 1921, in "Young India," his stirring rejoinder appears. Gandhi thanks the "Great Sentinel"[1] for having warned India as to the pitfalls ahead. He agrees with Tagore that most essential of all is the maintenance of a free spirit.

> We must not surrender our reason into anybody's keeping. Blind surrender to love is often more mischievous than forced surrender to the lash of the tyrant. There is hope for the slave of the brute, none for that of love.

Tagore is the sentinel who warns of the approach of the enemies called Bigotry, Lethargy, Intolerance, Ignorance, and Inertia. But Gandhi does not feel that Tagore's misgivings are justified. The Mahatma always appeals to reason. It is not true that India is moved by blind obedience only. If the country decided to adopt the spinning-wheel, this has been only after considerable reflection. Tagore speaks of patience and is satisfied with beautiful songs. But there is war. Let the poet lay down his lyre! Let him sing when it is over! When a house is on fire, *all* must go out and take up a bucket to quench the fire.

When all about me are dying for want of food, the only occupation permissible for me is to feed the hungry. India is a house on fire. It is dying of hunger because it has no work to buy food with. Khulna is starving. The Ceded Districts are passing successively through a fourth famine. Orissa is a land suffering

1. Title of the article of October 13, 1921.

from chronic famine. India is growing daily poorer. The circulation about her feet and legs has almost stopped. And if we do not take care she will collapse altogether...

To a people famishing and idle the only acceptable form in which God can dare appear is work and promise of food as wages. God created man to work for his food and said that those who ate without work were thieves. We must think of millions who to-day are less than animals, almost in a dying state. Hunger is the argument that is drawing India to the spinning-wheel.

The poet lives for the morrow, and would have us do likewise. He presents to our admiring gaze the beautiful picture of the birds in the early morning singing hymns of praise as they soar into the sky. Those birds had their day's food and soared with rested wings in whose veins new blood had flown the previous night. But I have had the pain of watching birds who for want of strength could not be coaxed even into a flutter of their wings. The human bird under the Indian sky gets up weaker than when he pretended to retire. For millions it is an eternal vigil or an eternal trance. I have found it impossible to soothe suffering patients with a song from Kabir...

Give them work that they may eat! "Why should I, who have no need to work for food, spin?" may be the question asked. Because I am eating what does not belong to me. I am living on the spoliation of my countrymen. Trace the course of every coin that finds its way into your pocket, and you will realize the truth of what I write. Everyone must spin. Let Tagore spin, like the others. Let him burn his foreign clothes; that is the duty to-day. God will take care of the morrow. As it says in the Gitâ, Do *right!*

Dark and tragic words these! Here we have the misery of the world rising up before the dream of art and crying, "Dare deny me existence!" Who does not sympathize with Gandhi's passionate emotion and share it?

And yet, in his reply so proud and so poignant, there is nevertheless something that justifies Tagore's misgivings: *sileat poeta*, imposing silence on the person who is called upon to obey the imperious discipline of the cause. Obey without discussion the law of *Swadeshi*, the first command of which is, Spin!

No doubt, in the human battle, discipline is a duty. But, unfortunately, those who are intrusted with enforcing this discipline, the master's lieutenants, may be narrow-minded men. They may mistake the discipline chosen to attain the ideal for the ideal itself. Discipline fascinates them by its rigidity, for they are of the kind who feel at ease only on the narrow path. They look upon *Swadeshi* as essential, not as a means to an end, but in itself. In their eyes it acquires an almost sacred character. One of Gandhi's disciples, professor at the school that lies nearest his heart, the *Satyagraha Ashram* of Sarbarmati at Ahmedabad, Mr. D. B. Kalelkar, writes a "Gospel of Swadeshi," which Gandhi, in a preface, stamps with his approval.[1] This book, or pamphlet, is addressed to the man in the street. Let us examine the creed as it is taught by one of those who drink at the very source of the unpolluted doctrine:

> Now and then God is incarnated on earth to redeem the world. His incarnation need not necessarily be in human form... He may be manifest in an abstract principle or in an ideal which uplifts the world... His latest incarnation is in the "Gospel of Swadeshi"...

1. "The Gospel of Swadeshi," Madras, 1922.

The apostle realizes that this statement may cause a smile if *Swadeshi* is to be interpreted as meaning the boycott of foreign goods only. This is only a partial application of *Swadeshi*, which is a "vast religious principle that will rid the world of strife and hatred and liberate humanity." Its quintessence may be found in the Indian scriptures:

> Your own religious *Dharma*—that is to say, your own religious destiny or salvation—though imperfect, is the best. The fulfilment of *Dharma* for which you were not intended is always fraught with danger. He alone attains happiness who fulfils the task laid out for him.

The fundamental law of *Swadeshi* springs from faith in God, "who has provided, in all eternity, for the happiness of the world. This God has placed each human being in the environment best suited for the fulfilment of his task. A man's work and his aspirations should be suited to his position in the world. We cannot choose our culture any more than our birth, family, or country. We must accept what God has given us; we must accept tradition as coming from God and regard it as a strict duty to live up to it. To renounce tradition would be sinful."

From these premises it follows that the inhabitant of one country should not concern himself with other countries.

> The follower of *Swadeshi* never takes upon himself the vain task of trying to reform the world, for he believes that the world is moved and always will be moved according to rules set by God... One must not expect the people of one country to provide for the needs of another, even for philanthropic reasons, and if it were possible, it would not be desirable... The true follower of *Swadeshi*

> does not forget that every human being is his brother, but that it is incumbent on him to fulfil the task his particular environment has laid down for him. Just as we must work out our salvation in the century in which we are born, we should serve the country in which we are born. The emancipation of our soul should be sought through religion and our own culture.

Is it, however, permissible for a nation to take advantage of all opportunities to develop its resources of commerce and industry? Indeed not. An unworthy ambition to wish to develop India's manufactures! It would be asking people to violate their *Dharmas!* It is as criminal to export one's products as to import those of others. "For proselytism is repellent to the spirit of *Swadeshi.*" And the logical conclusion of this theory, rather startling to a European, is that it is as sinful to export goods as ideas. If India has been bitterly humiliated in history, it is as punishment for the crimes of ancestors who traded with ancient Egypt and Rome, a crime deliberately repeated by all succeeding generations. Every nation, every class, should remain true to its own duty, live on its own resources, and be inspired by its own traditions.

> We should avoid being intimate with those whose social customs are different from ours. We should not mingle in the lives of men or peoples whose ideals are different from ours... Every man is a brook. Every nation is a river. They must follow their course, clear and pure, till they reach the Sea of Salvation, where all will blend.

What is this but the triumph of nationalism? The narrowest and most unpolluted? Stay at home, shut all doors, change nothing, hold on to everything, export nothing, buy nothing, uplift and purify body and spirit! A gospel, indeed, of medieval monks![1] And Gandhi, of the broad mind, lets his name be associated with it!

Tagore's bewilderment, when met with these visionaries of reactionary nationalism, is comprehensible. No wonder he was taken aback by these apostles, who would reverse the march of centuries, shut the free soul in a cage, and burn all bridges communicating with the West.[2] As a matter of fact, Gandhi's doctrine really implies nothing of the sort. As may be seen from his reply to Tagore, he says, "*Swadeshi* is a message to the world." The world exists; therefore, Gandhi reckons with it, and does not repudiate "proselyting. Non-coöperation," he says, "is not directed against the English or the West. Our non-coöperation is directed against material civilization and its attendant greed and exploitation of the weak." In other words, it combats the errors of

1. In this "Gospel," however, are words of great moral force and beauty. Exert no vengeance. "That which is passed is passed. The past cannot be called back; it is part of eternity and man has no recourse against it. Do not try to exert reprisals as punishment for past injustice and offence! Let the dead past bury its dead. Act in the living present, heart within and God o'erhead."

   The cold purity of the glaciers blows through the book, from one end to the other.

2. Tagore was particularly sensitive to such writings since there had sprung up a sort of rivalry between Gandhi's *Ashram* (where this "Gospel" was written) and Tagore's *Santiniketan*, a rivalry which both men tried to smooth out. In an article published February 9, 1922, Gandhi, in "Young India," complains that a journalist misquoted him, making him say things about his *Ashram* which might be construed as criticisms of Tagore's *Santiniketan*. Gandhi expresses his respect for Tagore's school and adds, rather humorously, that if he had to determine the superiority of one school over the other, he would vote for *Santiniketan*, in spite of the discipline of *Ashram*. *Santiniketan* is the older brother, older in age as well as in wisdom, but, says Gandhi, "Let the disciples of *Santiniketan* beware the growth of little *Ashram*!

the West and would therefore be beneficial to the West also. "Our non-coöperation is a retirement within ourselves." A temporary retirement to enable India to gather up her forces before placing them at the services of humanity. "India must learn to live before she can aspire to die for humanity." Gandhi does not forbid coöperation with Europe provided the sound ideal which he sets up for all men is adhered to.

Gandhi's real doctrine is much broader, much more human, much more universal[1] than that expressed in the "Gospel" which he has approved. Why did Gandhi lend his name to this "Gospel"? Why does he let his magnificent ideal, a message for the whole world, be imprisoned within the narrow bonds of an Indian theocracy? Beware of disciples! The purer they are, the more pernicious. God preserve a great man from friends who only grasp part of his ideal! In codifying it, they destroy the harmony which is the real blessing of his living soul.

But this is not all. While the disciples who live near the master are at least tinged by his noble spirituality, what about the disciples of his disciples, and the others, the masses to whom the doctrine comes merely as vague and broken echoes? How much and what do they absorb of the gospel of spiritual purification and creative renouncement? Unfortunately, to them the doctrine appears in its most rudimentary and material form, in a sort of

1. To my mind Gandhi is as universal as Tagore, but in a different way. Gandhi is a universalist through his religious feeling; Tagore is intellectually universal. Gandhi does not exclude anyone from the communion of prayer and daily duties, just as the first apostles did not differentiate between Jews and Gentiles but imposed the same moral discipline on both. This is what Gandhi aspires to do, and herein lies his narrowness; not in his heart, which is as large as that of a Christ, but in his spirit of intellectual asceticism and renunciation. (And this, too, is of a Christ!) Gandhi is a universalist of the Middle Ages. While venerating him, we understand and approve Tagore.

Messianic waiting for the advent of *Swaraj*, home rule, by the spinning-wheel! This is the negation of all progress. It's the old *fuori Barbari*. Tagore is alarmed, and not without reason, at the violence of the apostles of non-violence, and even Gandhi is not absolutely free from it. Gandhi says that he would "withdraw from the field if he felt hatred for the English," for one must love one's enemies while hating their deeds, "hate Satanism while loving Satan." The distinction, however, is a little too subtle for the average man to grasp. And when at each session of the congress the leaders dwell with fiery eloquence on the crimes and treachery of the English, anger and rancor pile up behind the sluices; and beware when the sluices burst! When Gandhi, explaining why he advocates the burning of precious stuffs in Bombay in August, 1921, says to Andrews, Tagore's friend, that "He is transferring ill will from men to things,"[1] he does not realize that the fury of the masses is gathering impetus, and that instinctively these masses reason, "Things first, men next!" He does not foresee that in this same Bombay, less than three months afterward, *men* will be killing *men*. Gandhi is too much of a saint; he is too pure, top free from the animal passions that lie dormant in man. He does not dream that they lie there, crouching within the people, devouring his words and thriving on them. Tagore, more clear-sighted, realizes the danger the non-coöperators are skirting when they innocently lay bare the crimes of Europe, profess non-violence, and simultaneously plant in people's minds the virus which will inevitably break in violence! But this they do not realize, these apostles whose hearts are free from hatred. But he who would lead men in action must know the heart-beats of the others, not merely his own. Beware the mob! *Cave canem!* The moral precepts of a Gandhi will not

1. September 1, 1921.

be able to curb it. The only way, perhaps, to prevent it from running wild, the only way, perhaps, of making it yield docilely to the austere discipline of the master, would be for him to pose as an incarnated god, as those who paint him as Sri-Krishna secretly hope he will do. But Gandhi's sincerity and his humility prevent him from playing the role.

And then, planning above the roaring human ocean alone, remains the single voice of the purest of men, but only a man. How long will it be heard? Grandiose and tragic waiting!

Part Three

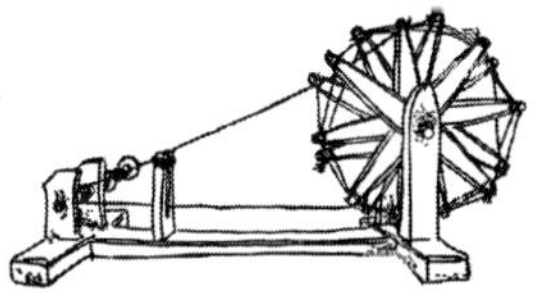

CHAPTER 1

In 1921 the non-coöperation movement evolved rapidly. The whole year was one of uncertainty, expectancy, and violent outbreaks. Gandhi inevitably reflected its oscillations.

For a long time hostility had been growing, and it broke out in open revolt at the Government's brutally oppressive measures. There were riots at Malegaon, in the district of Nasik, and at Giridih, in Behar. In the beginning of May, 1921, there were serious clashes in Assam. Twelve thousand coolies stopped work in the tea-gardens, and were attacked by Gurkhas drafted by the Government, and in eastern Bengal the railroad and steamship workers organized a two months' strike in protest. Gandhi did all in his power to calm the effervescence. In May he had a long conversation with the viceroy, Lord Reading, and he also used his influence with the Ali brothers, who were said to be stirring up violence by their inflammatory speeches. Gandhi was able to persuade his Moslem friends to "refrain from directly or indirectly advocating violence."

The non-coöperation movement, however, grew more and more powerful as time went on. The Moslem element in particular became audacious. At Karachi, July 8, for instance, the All-India Khilafat Conference, after reiterating the Moslem claims, declared that no Mussulman should serve in the English Army or assist in recruiting. In fact, the conference even went so far as to threaten to proclaim a republic in India and advocate civil disobedience at the December session of the National Congress if the Government did not change its hostile attitude to the Angora leaders. A little later, on July 28, the committee of the National Congress (the first congress committee elected according to the new constitution) sitting at Bombay decided to boycott the Prince of Wales, whose visit was announced, and declared a boycott on all foreign materials, to become effective before September 30. It also took steps to intensify and regulate national spinning and weaving, and urged the organization of a more vigorous campaign against the drink evil, despite the Government's support of the dealers. Less audacious than the Mussulmans of the Khilafat Conference, however, the congress committee disavowed revolutionary tendencies and disapproved civil disobedience, approving a more; strenuous propaganda in favor of non-violence.

In August a brutal revolt of the Moplahs took place, and lasted several months. With Maulana Mohamed Ali, Gandhi decided to go from Calcutta to Malabar to try to quiet it. But the Government arrested Maulana Mohamed and his brother Maulana Shaukat Ali as well as several other Moslem notables, accusing them of having voted for civil disobedience at the Khilafat Conference. At the news of the Ali brothers' arrest, the Central Khilafat Committee, sitting at Delhi, ratified unanimously the resolutions of the Khilafat Conference. Hundreds of demonstrations, held all over India, confirmed the people's approval of them. On October 4, Gandhi announced that he considered his cause hound up with that of the Mussulmans. In a manifesto approved by fifty prominent members of the All-India Congress Gandhi declared that every citizen was entitled to express his views on non-coöperation, adding that no Indian, whether civil functionary or soldier, should serve a Government which has brought about the moral, political, and economical degradation of India. He set up non-coöperation with such a Government as an imperative duty. The Ali brothers' trial took place at Karachi. With their fellow-accused, they were sentenced to two years' imprisonment.

To this sentence India replied with redoubled vigor. Gandhi's manifesto was ratified by the Committee of the All-India Congress on November 4 at Delhi. And casting the die, the committee authorized every province, on its own responsibility, to proclaim civil disobedience, beginning with a refusal to pay taxes. "Resisters," however, were first to swear complete obedience to the *Swadeshi* program, including hand spinning, and take the vow of non-violence. In other words, under Gandhi's direction the committee tried to combine resistance against the Government with discipline and self-sacrifice. To make the disinterested character of the movement clear. Resisters were informed that neither they nor their families would receive any pecuniary aid from the committee.

The great disobedience was about to become effective when, on November 17, the Prince of Wales landed at Bombay. The boycott was carried out by the lower and the middle classes; but the rich, the Parsees and official personages, ignored the order completely. Their attitude created such fury among the populace that the masses stormed the houses of the rich, looting and sacking homes and property, sparing no one, not even the women. Many were killed and wounded. This was the only case of violence, however. Everywhere else, all over India, the prescribed *hartal* took place in the midst of almost religious quiet and order. There were no disturbances of any kind. But the news of the Bombay riots wounded Gandhi "like an arrow shot in his heart." As soon as he heard of them he rushed to the spot, and when the rioters cheered him his mortification knew no bounds. He called the crowd angrily to order and commanded it to disperse. He declared that the Parsees were justified in celebrating the prince's arrival if they wished, and, in any event, nothing justified violence. The crowd listened to Gandhi in silence, but farther off the tumult broke out again. The worst elements seemed to have suddenly emerged from the earth, and twenty thousand men, towering in rage and hatred, cannot be brought back to reason all at once. Still, the rioters remained localized in certain districts, and the destruction was not half so great as that caused by the most insignificant revolutionary outbreak in Europe. Gandhi, however, issued anguished appeals to the citizens of Bombay and to the non-coöperators, and declared that such incidents proved that the masses were not yet ripe for civil disobedience. Therefore he suspended the order proclaiming it. To punish himself for the violence of his followers, he imposed upon himself a religious fast of twenty-four hours every week.

The European residents in India were less alarmed by the Bombay riots than by the striking unanimousness of the silent *hartal* throughout the country. They urged the viceroy and the Government to act, and a series of oppressive measures were imposed in the various provinces. An old law, aimed at anarchists and secret societies, dating from the uprisings of 1908, was unearthed, and made to serve against the volunteer associations of the Congress and of the Khilafat. Arrests were made by the thousand, which only resulted in bringing thousands of new recruits to register as volunteers, who were then trained by the provincial committees. In the meantime a *hartal* was set for December 24, the date of the Prince of Wales's visit to Calcutta. That day the prince passed through a silent, absolutely deserted city.

The revolution seemed to be smoldering everywhere, ready to burst into flame when the Indian National Congress met at Ahmedabad. There was about it the impressive solemnity of the États-Généraux on the eve of the French Revolution in 1789. The president of the congress had just been imprisoned. The discussions were brief. The congress again proclaimed its faith in non-coöperation and invited all citizens to register as volunteers and to be prepared to face arrest. It also urged the people to organize mass-meetings everywhere; and after expressing the opinion that civil disobedience is a weapon equally effective and more humane than armed rebellion, it moved that civil disobedience be adopted as soon as the masses had grasped the real spirit of non-violence. Realizing that many of the members would be arrested at the close of the session, the congress delegated its powers to Gandhi, investing him with a dictature *de facto* and authorizing him to appoint his successor. This made Gandhi sole master of India's policy. The congress limited his authority on one point only, and this was that he should agree to no change in the national *creed* nor make peace with the Government without the consent of the congress committee. A fraction of the assembly tried to pass a resolution approving violence, if necessary to bring about India's independence, but this resolution was rejected by the majority, which believed in Gandhi's principles.

The ensuing weeks revealed the religious enthusiasm which swept over India. Twenty-five thousand men and women joyfully surrendered themselves to prison guards. And back of them, thousands of others stood ready to give themselves up to prove their faith in the cause of India.

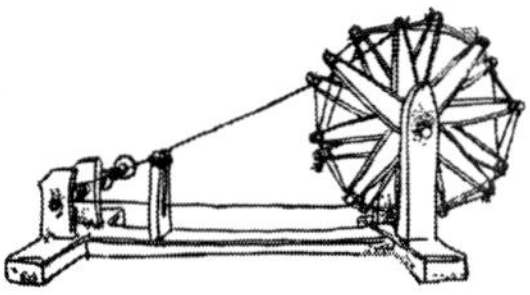

CHAPTER 2

Again Gandhi believed the country was ripe for civil disobedience *en masse.* The signal was to be given in a model district, at Bardoli, in the province of Bombay.[1] Here Gandhi's ideas had always been understood and followed. In an open letter to the viceroy, dated February 9, 1922, Gandhi set forth his program. The letter is a courteous, but clear, declaration of war. Gandhi says he is the leader of the non-coöperation movement, and he claims responsibility for it. Bardoli will be the first unit of non-violent mass revolt against a government which has brutally infringed upon freedom of the press, of association, and of speech. Gandhi gives Lord Reading seven days in which to announce a change of policy. If the "viceroy will not or cannot see such an incredibly simple issue," civil disobedience will be proclaimed.[2]

Scarcely had the letter, to the viceroy been despatched when there occurred an outbreak more violent than any of the others. During a procession at Chauri-Chaura, in the district of Gorakhpur,

1. One hundred and forty villages, 87,000 inhabitants.
2. A note in "Young India" of the same date is even more explicit. If the viceroy does not answer, civil obedience will be proclaimed even if against the will of the majority.

or, rather, after the procession had passed, some stragglers were "interfered with and abused by the constables." Attacked by the mob, the constables opened fire, and when they exhausted their ammunition they retired to the *thana* (the police barracks) for safety. The mob set fire to the *thana.* In vain the besieged begged for mercy. They were pitilessly massacred and burned. As the provocation had come from them, however, and as no non-coöperation volunteer had had a hand in the attack, Gandhi would have been justified in disclaiming all responsibility for the outrage. But he had really become the conscience of India. The crime of a single one of his people cut him to the quick. He took upon himself all the sins of his people. His horror was such that on the spur of the moment, and for the second time, he stopped the civil-disobedience movement that he had just launched. The situation was vastly more complicated than after the Bombay riots, and only a few days before he had sent his ultimatum to the viceroy. How could he retract it without making his program seem illogical and even ridiculous? "Satan," as Gandhi says, "forbade it." Realizing that "Satan's" voice was the voice of *pride*, he decided to retract the manifesto.

And on February 16, 1922, there appeared in "Young India" one of the most extraordinary human documents ever written. It is Gandhi's *mea culpa*, his public confession. From the depths of his mortification words of thanks swell to his lips, of thanks to God for having humbled him:

> God has been abundantly kind to me. He has warned me for the third time that there is not as yet in India that truthful and non-violent atmosphere which, and which alone, can justify mass disobedience, which can be at all described as "civil," which means gentle, truthful, humble,

> knowing, wilful, yet loving, never criminal and hateful. He warned me in 1919 when the Rowlatt Act agitation was started. Ahmedabad, Viramvrag, and Kheda erred. I retraced my steps, called it a Himalayan miscalculation, humbled myself before God and man, and stopped not merely mass civil disobedience, but even my own... The next time it was through the events of Bombay that God gave me a terrific warning. He made me eyewitness... I announced my intention to stop the mass civil disobedience which was to be immediately started in Bardoli. The humiliation was greater than that in 1919. But it did me good and I am sure that the nations gained by the stopping. India stood for truth and non-violence by the suspension.
>
> But the bitterest humiliation was still to come... God spoke clearly through Chauri-Chaura... And when India claims to be non-violent and hopes to mount the throne of liberty through non-violent means, mob violence even in answer to grave provocation is a bad augury... Non-violent attainment of self-government presupposes a non-violent control over the violent elements in the country. Non-violent non-coöperators can only succeed when they have succeeded in attaining control over the hooligan of India...

Therefore, on February 11, at Bardoli, he "put his doubts and troubles" before the working committee of the congress. They did not all agree with him. "But never," he said, "has a man been 'blessed,' perhaps, with colleagues and associates so considerate and forgiving."

They sympathized with his scruples and consented, at his request, to suspend the order of civil disobedience, urging at the same time that all organizations strive to create an atmosphere of non-violence.

> I know that the drastic reversal of practically the whole of the aggressive program may be politically unsound and unwise, but there is no doubt that it is religiously sound. The country will have gained by my humiliation and confession of error. The only virtue I want to claim is truth and non-violence. I lay no claim to superhuman powers. I want none. I wear the same corruptible flesh that the weakest of my fellow-beings wear, and am therefore as liable to err as any. My services have many limitations, but God has up to now blessed them in spite of the imperfections.
>
> For confession of error is like a broom that sweeps away dirt and leaves the surface cleaner and brighter. I feel stronger for my confession. And the cause must prosper for the retracing. Never has a man reached his destination by persistence in deviation from the straight path. It has been urged that Chauri-Chaura cannot affect Bardoli... I have no doubt whatsoever on that account. The people of Bardoli are, in my opinion, the most peaceful in India. But Bardoli is but a speck on the map of India. Its effort cannot succeed unless there is perfect coöperation from the other parts... Just as the addition of a grain of arsenic to a pot of milk renders it unfit as food so will the civility of Bardoli prove unacceptable by the addition of the deadly poison from Chauri-Chaura... The latter represents India as much as Bardoli. Chauri-Chaura is,

after all, an aggravated symptom. *In civil disobedience there should be no excitement. Civil disobedience is a preparation for mute suffering.* Its effect is marvelous, though unperceived and gentle... The tragedy of Chauri-Chaura is really the index-finger. It shows the way India may easily go if drastic precautions be not taken. If we are not to evolve violence out of non-violence, it is quite clear that we must hastily retrace our steps and reestablish an atmosphere of peace, and not think of starting mass civil disobedience until we are sure of peace being retained in spite of mass civil disobedience being started and in spite of government provocation... Let the opponent glory in our humiliation and so-called defeat. It is better to be charged with cowardice than to be guilty of denial of our oath and sin against God...

And the apostle wants to redeem the bloodshed by others:

I must undergo personal cleansing. I must become a fitter instrument able to register the slightest variation in the moral atmosphere about me. My prayers must have deeper truth and humility. For me there is nothing so cleansing as a fast. A fast undertaken for fuller self-expression, for attainment of the spirit's supremacy over the flesh, is a most powerful factor in one's evolution...[1]

And he imposes on himself a continuous five days' fast. He does not want his co-workers to follow his example. He must punish himself. "I am in the unhappy position of a surgeon proved skill-less to deal with an admittedly dangerous case. I must

1. What light these words throw on the mysterious power of this soul where all the emotions of hit people are inscribed!

either abdicate or acquire greater skill." His fast is penance and punishment for him and for the rioters of Chauri-Chaura who signed with his name on their lips. Gandhi would like to suffer for them alone, but he advises them to hand themselves voluntarily to the Government and to make a clean confession, for they have injured the cause they meant to serve.

> I would suffer humiliation, every torture, absolute ostracism, and death itself to prevent the movement from becoming violent or a precursor of violence.

The history of humanity's spiritual progress can point to few pages as noble as these. The moral value of such an action is incomparable, but as a political move it was disconcerting. Gandhi himself admits it might be called "politically unsound and unwise." It is dangerous to assemble all the forces of a nation and to hold the nation, panting, before a prescribed movement, to lift one's arm to give the final command, and then, at the last moment, let one's arm drop and thrice call a halt just as the formidable machinery has been set in motion. One risks ruining the brakes and paralyzing the impetus.

Therefore, when the congress committee held its session at Delhi, February 24, 1922, Gandhi met with great opposition. The resolutions of the working committee of Bardoli, approved on the eleventh, were not ratified without discussion. The non-coöperators split into two camps. Gandhi claimed that before civil disobedience could be launched the people must be better prepared, and he submitted a constructive program. But many members were irritated at the slow progress of the independence movement, and they protested against the suspension of civil disobedience. Gandhi's methods, they claimed, were stifling the nation's ardor. A vote of censure against the working committee was proposed, and it was suggested that its resolutions be annulled. In the end, however, Gandhi triumphed. But he suffered keenly, for he realized that the majority was not backing him sincerely; he knew that more than one of those who voted for him called him "dictator" behind his back. He knew that, at bottom, he no longer reflected the sentiment of the country. And with his undaunted sincerity he admits this, March 2, 1922:

> There is so much undercurrent of violence, both conscious and unconscious, that I was actually and literally praying for a disastrous defeat. I have always been in a minority. In South Africa I started with practical unanimity, reached a minority of sixty-four and even sixteen, and went up again to a huge majority. The best and the most solid work was done in the wilderness of minority... I know that the only thing that the Government dreads is this huge majority I seem to command. They little know that I dread it even more than they. I have become literally sick of the adoration of the unthinking multitude. I would feel certain of my ground if I was spat upon by them. A friend warned me against exploiting my "dictatorship." I have begun to wonder if I am not unconsciously allowing myself to be "exploited"! I confess that I have a dread of it as I never had before. My only safety lies in my shamelessness. I have warned my friends of the committee that I am incorrigible. I shall continue to confess blunders each time the people commit them. The only tyrant I accept in this world is the "still small voice" within. And even though I have to face the prospect of a minority of one, I humbly believe I have the courage

to be in such a hopeless minority. That to me is the only truthful position. But I am a sadder and, I hope, a wiser man to-day. I see that our non-violence is skin-deep. We are burning with indignation. The Government is feeding it by its insensate acts. It seems almost as if the Government wants to see this land covered with murder, arson, and rapine in order to be able once more to claim exclusive ability to put them down.

This non-violence, therefore, seems to be due merely to our helplessness. It almost appears as if we are nursing in our bosoms the desire to take revenge the first time we get the opportunity. Can true voluntary non-violence come out of this seeming forced non-violence of the weak? Is it not a futile experiment I am conducting? What if, when the fury bursts, not a man, woman, or child is safe and every man's hand is raised against his fellow-being? Of what avail is it, then, if I fast myself to death in the event of such a catastrophe coming to pass? Let us be truthful. If it is by force that we wish to gain *Swaraj*, let us drop non-violence and offer such violence as we may. It would be a manly, honest, and sober attitude, and no one can then accuse us of the terrible charge of hypocrisy.[1] If, in spite of all my warnings... the majority did not believe in our goal, although they accepted it without a single material change, I would ask them to realize their responsibility. They are not bound

1. Gandhi had come to realize that some of the majority members who voted for non-violence looked upon it, in their hearts, as a political expedient paving the way, covertly, to violence. They spoke suavely, he says, "of delivering non-violent blows." Gandhi had not grasped the danger, as Tagore had, long before. But he was horror-struck. And, more harshly than Tagore, he denounced and attacked the majority's attitude.

to rush to civil disobedience, but to settle down to the quiet work of construction. If we do not take care, we are likely to be drowned in the waters whose depth we do not know...

Those who do not believe in the creed should surely retire from the congress.

And, turning to the minority, Gandhi adds:

The patriotic spirit demands loyal and strict adherence to non-violence and truth. Those who do not believe in them should retire from the congress organization.

There is bitter sadness, but a proud manliness, in these forceful words. It was the night in Gethsemane. Gandhi's arrest was imminent. Who knows whether, in his heart, he did not look upon imprisonment as a delivery?

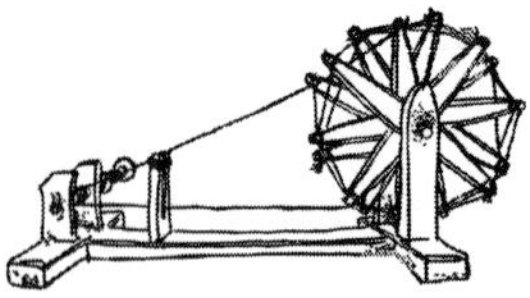

CHAPTER 3

Gandhi had for a long time been expecting to be arrested. Ever since November 10, 1920, all his affairs had been in order and he himself prepared. He had dictated his instructions to the people in his article, "If I Am Arrested." He referred to this possibility again in an article dated March 9, 1922, when the rumor of his arrest again cropped up. He says he does not fear the Government. "Rivers of bloodshed by the Government cannot frighten me." The only thing he fears is that the people may be carried away at the news of his arrest. This would be a disgrace to him. "I desire that the people should maintain perfect self-control and consider the day of my arrest a day of rejoicing. The Government believes that I am the soul of all this agitation and that if I am removed it will be left in peace. The only thing that remains is for it to measure the strength of the people. Let the people preserve perfect peace and calmness. It is a matter of no pride or pleasure to me, but of humiliation, that the Government refrain from arresting me for fear of an outbreak of universal violence." Let the people carry out the whole constructive program. Let there be no *hartals* or demonstrations, no cooperation with the Government. Let courts and schools be boycotted. Let, in short, the program of non-coöperation be pursued in absolute order and discipline. If the people can live up to this program, they will win. Otherwise they will face disaster.

When everything was in readiness, Gandhi went to his cherished retreat at the *Ashram* of Sarbarmati, near Ahmedabad, to await, in quiet meditation and surrounded by his beloved disciples, the coming of the constables. He longed for imprisonment. In his absence India would affirm her purpose with greater strength. And, as he says, imprisonment would give him "a quiet and physical rest," which he perhaps deserved.[1]

The constables arrived on the night of March 10. News had reached the *Ashram* of their coming. The Mahatma was ready, and placed himself at their disposal. On the way to prison he met Maulana Hasrat Mohani, a Mohammedan friend who had come from far to give him a last embrace. Banker, the editor of "Young India," was sent to jail along with the master. Gandhi's wife was allowed to accompany her husband as far as the prison gates.

At noon of Saturday, March 18, Gandhi's "Great Trial"[2] began before Mr. C. N. Broomsfield, district and session judge of Ahmedabad. It was a manifestation of rare nobility and high-mindedness. Judge and accused vied with each other in chivalrous courtesy. Never in the struggle did England rise to more magnanimous impartiality. Judge Broomsfield that day made up for many faults of the Government. Since much has been written about the trial, I will only summarize the main points.

Why had the Government at last arrested Gandhi? Why, after contemplating this move for more than two years, did it choose

---

1. March 9, 1922.
2. "The Great Trial, Young India," March 23, 1922.

the very moment when the Mahatma had quelled the mob movement and when he seemed to stand as the only barrier against violence? Was it acting in aberration? Or did it wish to lend confirmation to Gandhi's terrible words: "It seems almost as if the Government wants to see this land covered with murder, arson, and rapine in order to be able to claim exclusive ability to put them down"? The Government was in a very difficult position. It respected and feared Gandhi. It would have liked to treat him gently. But Gandhi did not treat the Government gently. The Mahatma condemned violence, but his non-violence was more revolutionary than any violence. The very same day that he stopped civil disobedience for the mass, or rather the day before the session of the congress at Delhi, on February 23, he wrote one of the most menacing articles to Great Britain's power. An insolent telegram from Lord Birkenhead and Mr. Montagu had struck India as a blow.[1]

In a burst of indignation Gandhi took up the challenge:

> How can there be any compromise whilst the British lion continues to shake his gory claws in our faces? The British Empire, which is based upon organized exploitation of physically weaker races and upon a continuous exhibition of brute force, cannot live if there is a just God ruling the universe... It is high time that the British people were made to realize that the fight that was commenced in 1920 is a fight to the finish, whether it lasts one month

1. "If the existence of our Empire were challenged, the discharge of responsibilities of the British Government to India prevented and demands were made in the very mistaken belief that we contemplated retreat from India, then India would not challenge with success the most determined people in the world who once again would answer with all the vigor and determination at its command."

> of one year or many months or many years. I shall only hope and pray that God will give India sufficient humility and sufficient strength to remain non-violent to the end. Submission to the insolent challenges that are cabled is now an utter impossibility.

Gandhi was indicted on the statements contained in this article and in two other articles, the one dated September 19, 1921, and the other December 15, 1921. The first referred to the arrest of the Ali brothers, and the second was a reply to a speech of Lord Reading. Both of them contain the same declaration of "fight to the finish. We want *Swaraj*, we want the Government to yield to popular will. We ask for no quarter and expect none." The accusation, therefore, charged that Gandhi had "preached disaffection toward the Government and had openly instigated others to overthrow it." Gandhi spoke in his own defense. He pleaded guilty to all charges.

The advocate-general, Sir J. T. Strangman of Bombay, claimed that the three articles cited by the accusation were not isolated, but were part of a general campaign pursued for two years in view of overthrowing the Government, and he quoted passages from Gandhi's articles. He paid tribute to Gandhi's high character. But this only served to lend authority to the articles and to increase their harmful influence. He held Gandhi responsible for the bloodshed at Bombay and at Chauri-Chaura. It was true that Gandhi preached non-violence, but he also preached disaffection. He was therefore responsible for the violence committed by the people.

Gandhi asked permission to speak. The torment as to what was right and wrong, the anguish, the doubts, the mental and spiritual struggle of the last weeks as to which course he should pursue and the effect it would have on the people, had been cleared away. He had recovered the serenity of his soul. He accepted everything that had taken place and everything that was to take place as a necessity which he might regret, but which he would have to bear. He agreed with the advocate-general. Yes, he was responsible. He was responsible for everything. He had preached disaffection for a much longer time than the accusation had stated. He assumed responsibility for the troubles at Madras, for the "diabolical crimes" of Chauri-Chaura, and the "mad outrages" of Bombay.

> The learned advocate-general is quite right when he says that as a man of responsibility, a man having received a fair share of education, having had a fair share of experience of this world, I should have known the consequences of every one of my acts. *I knew that I was playing with fire, I ran the risk, and if I was set free, I would still do the same.* I felt this morning that I would have failed in my duty if I did not say what I say here just now.
>
> I wanted to avoid violence, I want to avoid violence. Non-violence is the first article of my faith. It is also the last article of my creed. But I had to make my choice. I had either to submit to a system which I considered had done an irreparable harm to my country or incur the risk of the mad fury of my people bursting forth when they understood the truth from my lips. I know that my people have sometimes gone mad. I am deeply sorry for it and I am therefore here to submit not to a light penalty, but to the highest penalty. I do not ask for mercy. I do not plead any extenuating act. I am here, therefore, to invite and cheerfully submit to the highest penalty that

can be inflicted upon me for what in law is a deliberate crime and what appears to me to be the highest duty of a citizen. The only course open to you, Judge, is either to resign your post or inflict on me the severest penalty.

After this powerful improvisation, where the scruples of a religious spirit are balanced by the heroic firmness of a political leader, Gandhi read a written declaration addressed to the public in India and England. He owed it to them, he said, to explain why, "from a staunch loyalist and coöperator," he had become an uncompromising disaffectionist and non-coöperator. He dwelt on his public life from 1893 on. He pointed out all he had to suffer, as an Indian, from the British system, and he told of his ceaseless attempts for twenty-five years to reform it. He believed obstinately that this could be accomplished without separating India and England. In spite of all deceptions, he remained a stanch coöperator till 1919. But since then outrages and crimes have surpassed all measure. And instead of making up for injustices, the Government, as if in defiance to the spirit of India, has honored, pensioned, and rewarded its guilty servants. The Government itself has severed all ties. Gandhi has come to the conclusion that even if the desired reforms were now proposed by the Government, they would be harmful. The Government in British India is based on the exploitation of the masses. Laws are made in view of strengthening this exploitation. The administration of the law is prostituted consciously or unconsciously for the benefit of the exploiter. A subtle, but effective, system of terrorization and an organized display of force have emasculated the people and "induced in them the habit of simulation." India is starving, ruined, degraded; and many claim that before India becomes capable of self-government on the dominion plan generations will have to pass. England has done more harm to India than any previous system. Non-coöperation with evil is a duty. Gandhi' has done his duty. But whereas in the past non-coöperation has been deliberately expressed in the form of violence inflicted on the evildoer, violence having been the supreme weapon, Gandhi has given his people the new, but indomitable, arm of non-violence.

And then came the chivalrous match between Judge Broomsfield and the Mahatma.

> Mr. Gandhi, you have made my task easy in one way by pleading guilty to the charges; nevertheless what remains, namely the determination of a just sentence, is perhaps as difficult a proposition as a judge in this country could have to face... It would be impossible to ignore the fact that in the eyes of millions of your countrymen you are a great patriot and a great leader. Even those who differ from you in politics look upon you as a man of high ideals and of noble and even saintly life... But it is my duty to judge you as a man subject to the law... There are probably few people in India who do not sincerely regret that you should have made it impossible for any Government to leave you at liberty. But it is so. I am trying to balance what is due to you against what appears to me to be necessary in the interest of the public.

With great courtesy he consulted the accused as to the sentence which should be imposed. "You will not consider it unreasonable, I think, to be classed with Mr. Tilak," sentenced twelve years previously to six years. "If the course of events in India should make it possible for the Government to reduce the period and release you, no one will be better pleased than I."

Gandhi did not allow the judge to outdo him in courtesy. He claimed it was his proudest privilege and honor to have his name associated with that of Tilak. So far as the sentence itself was concerned, he considered it as light as any judge could impose on him, and as far as the whole proceedings were concerned, he said that he could not have expected greater courtesy.[1]

The trial was over. Gandhi's friends fell at his feet, sobbing. The Mahatma took leave of them, smiling. And the door of the jail of Sarbamati closed behind him.[2]

1. Mr. Banker, the editor of "Young India," who, during the trial, had followed the master's example and acquiesced in all his statements, was sentenced to a fine and imprisonment for one year.
2. Mrs. Kasturibai Gandhi informed the people of India of the sentence imposed on Gandhi, in a very beautiful message, urging them in peace and quiet to concentrate on carrying out Gandhi's constructive program.

   Gandhi did not remain in the prison of Sarbamati, where he was well treated, but was transferred to an unknown jail and then to Yeravda, near Poona. According to a statement made by N. D. Hardiker, "Gandhi in Prison, Unity," May 18, 1922, which we are unable to verify, Gandhi has been placed in a cell like the common-law criminals, and is allowed no privileges of any kind. It is claimed that his delicate health has suffered through this regime.

   "Mr. C. F. Andrews, speaking of Gandhi's imprisonment, told me that the Mahatma was happy in prison and that he had asked his friends not to visit him. He is purifying himself, he prays and feels convinced that in this way he is working in the most efficacious way for India."

   Incidentally Mr. Andrews states that the Gandhist party in India has gained strength by the Mahatma's imprisonment. India believes in Gandhi with more fervor than ever before. It persists in looking upon him as an incarnation of Sri-Krishna, who was also subjected to the trial of imprisonment. And Gandhi, in jail, has more effectively prevented the explosion of that violence which he feared than if he had been at liberty.

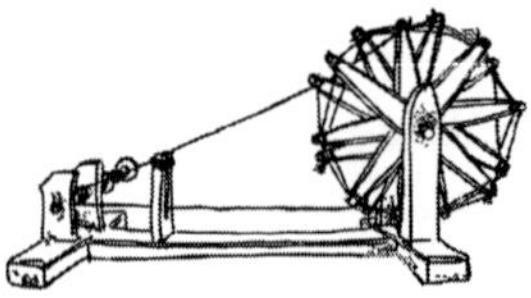

CHAPTER 4

Ever since the great apostle's voice has been silent. His body is walled in as in a tomb. But never did a tomb act as a barrier to thought, and Gandhi's invisible soul still animates India's vast body. "Peace, non-violence, suffering,"[1] is the only message that has come from the prison. The message has been heard. From one end of the country to the other the watchword has been passed. Three years earlier India would have been swept by bloodshed at Gandhi's arrest. The mere report of its having taken place caused riots among the population in 1920. But the sentence of Ahmedabad was received with religious solemnity. Thousands of Indians with serene joyfulness handed themselves over to prison guards. Non-violence and suffering—one example more amazing than the others—may serve to show to what depths the divine words have penetrated into the spirit of the nation.

1. On August 3, 1922, "Unity" published a "Letter from Prison" where Gandhi speaks about the evils of modern civilization. The letter seems apocryphal to me. I should imagine it a summary of extracts written some time ago, particularly in the "Hind Swaraj."

As is well known, the Sikhs have always been looked upon as one of the most warlike races in India. Large numbers of them served in the army during the war. Last year grave dissensions arose among them. To our Western eyes the cause seems insignificant. As the result of a religious effervescence, one of the Sikh sects, the Akalis, wished to purify the sanctuaries. The latter had fallen into the hands of guardians of ill repute who refused to be put out. For legal reasons the Government took their defense. And in August, 1922, began the daily martyrdom of Guru-Ka-Bagh.[1] The Akalis adopted the doctrine of non-resistance. A thousand of them settled near the sanctuary, while four thousand took up abode in the Golden Temple at Amritsar, ten miles away. Every day one hundred from among the four thousand, most of them men of military age, many of whom served in the war, left the Golden Temple, after taking the vow of remaining true to the principles of non-violence in thought as well as action, and of reaching Guru-Ka-Bagh or being brought back unconscious. Among the group of the thousand volunteers twenty-five made the same vow every day. Not far from the sanctuary the British constables waited at the bridge with iron-tipped rods to stop the manifestation. And every day a gruesome scene took place. Andrews, Tagore's friend, describes it unforgettably in his "Akali Struggle."[2] With a wreath of small white flowers around their black turbans, the Akalis arrived silently before the constables, and at a distance of about a yard they stopped and began to pray, silently, motionlessly. The constables, in order to drive them away, prodded them with the iron-tipped rods, jabbing harder and harder till blood began to flow and the Sikhs fell unconscious.

1. Guru-Ka-Bagh is a sanctuary (Gurdwara) about ten miles from Amritsar.
2. "The Akali Struggle," by Andrews, professor at Santiniketan. Published in the "Swaraiya" of Madras and under separate cover. September 1, 1922.

Those who could get to their feet would begin to pray again, until they were beaten into unconsciousness like the others. Andrews did not hear a single cry, nor did he see a defiant glance. Near-by, a crowd of spectators, their faces tense with anguish, prayed silently. "I could not help thinking," Andrews says, "of the shadow of the cross." The English described the scene in their papers and expressed amazement.[1] It seemed incomprehensible to the British, although they had to admit that the absurd sacrifice proved that the idea of non-coöperation and non-violence was gaining ground and that the people of the Punjab had been won over to the doctrine. Andrews, whose generous spirit and pure idealism enabled him to penetrate the soul of India, says that here he saw, like Goethe at Valmy, "the dawn of a new era. A new heroism, steeled by suffering, has risen, a *war of the spirit.*"

It would seem as if the people of India have lived up to Mahatma's spirit more faithfully than those whose mission it was to guide them. I have already spoken of the opposition to Gandhi at the session of the congress committee at Delhi twenty days before the master was arrested. This opposition still manifested itself when the committee met again, at Lucknow, June 7, 1922. The program of patient waiting and silent reconstruction advocated by Gandhi was bitterly criticized, and a motion was made to proclaim civil disobedience. A commission was appointed to inquire into conditions and determine whether the country might be called ripe for civil disobedience. The commission traveled all over India, and in the autumn sent in a discouraging report. Not only was civil disobedience called impractical for the present, but half the members went to such extremes of

1. "Manchester Guardian Weekly," October 13, 1922.

conservatism as to suggest that Gandhi's methods of non-coöperation be abandoned and a new *Swaraj* or home rule party be formed within the government councils. Gandhi's doctrine was, in other words, attacked by those who believed in violence, as well as by those who believed in prudence.

India, however, did not accept the commission's report. In its annual meeting at the end of December, 1922, the National Indian Congress energetically proclaimed its allegiance to the persecuted master and his doctrine of non-coöperation. By 1740 votes to 890 it rejected all participation in government councils. As for those who believed in violence, they were few and far between and had little influence. The session closed with a unanimous resolution urging that the political strike ordered by Gandhi be kept up. A resolution boycotting English materials, however, was turned down, in order not to antagonize European workmen. But the Mussulman conference of the Khilafat, as usual more audacious than the congress, voted for the boycott by a large majority.

Here we must stop the record of the Gandhist movement. Despite a few inevitable backslides due to the absence of the master and his best disciples, imprisoned like himself (especially the Ali brothers), the movement has successfully passed through the trials of the first unguided year. And the English press, at the close of the session of the congress of 1922 at Gaya, expresses surprise and disappointment at the progress of the movement.[1]

---

1. An article by Blanche Watson, in "Unity," November 16, 1922, enumerates the advantages which India has won by her fight of non-violent resistance.

This article claims that the internal revenues of India have decreased some seventy million dollars, and that the boycott of English goods has caused England to lose, in the course of a single year, some twenty million dollars. She claims that at that time about thirty thousand Indians were imprisoned, and that the governmental machinery was entirely upset. But Blanche Watson, who is a fervent admirer of Gandhism, has, perhaps, an unconscious tendency to exaggerate its successes. Other testimony would seem to be less encouraging and would seem to prove that the spirit of self-sacrifice is backed by the selfish attitude of the wealthy and of business people, while many of those who resigned from government posts in the first flush of enthusiasm have now returned to work. It would not be human to believe anything else. In every revolution many lag on behind, or retrace their steps. The point is to determine whether, or not, on the whole, the movement is on the increase or the decrease. In this connection it is interesting to refer to a description published in the "Manchester Guardian Weekly," February 16, 1928.

The "Manchester Guardian," whose intelligent liberalism is well known, but which nevertheless represents certain powerful interests directly imperiled by the non-coöperation movement, recently organized an investigation of conditions in India. The conclusion one draws after reading the results of this inquiry, in spite of a very natural tendency to discredit the movement, is that the situation is serious and causes grave misgivings. The last article (February 16, 1923) tries to prove that Gandhi's tactics have been proved ineffective and that the non-coöperation movement must be reorganized. But the article goes on to say that the spirit of non-coöperation is growing. Everywhere there are traces of distrust of the foreign Government and ardent hope of getting rid of it. The most cultivated people in India and the inhabitants of the large cities agree on this point. The *ryot*, or peasant, is only slightly affected by the movement, but conditions are such in the villages that within a short time he will have to take sides. The army still seems immune, but recruits come from the villages, and sooner or later they will be contaminated. The non-coöperation movement is frequently most intense among the best and the most moderate elements. These elements disapprove revolutionary methods, but their disapproval is not shared by the rest of the country. The writer claims that it will take about ten years for India really to bring about effective civil disobedience. But in the meantime the situation will grow more and more serious. It is impossible to hold the Indians in check by threatening them with imprisonment. They no longer fear it. Harsher coercive measures must be resorted to, and this will stir up hatred. There is only one peaceful solution—if it is not already too late—and that is for England to take the initiative of making Indian reforms. No half-measures, like those of 1919, and not applied till last year! They are not sufficient, and there is no time to lose. England must call a National Indian Convention where all parties and interests in India will be represented—Gandhi and his disciples as well as Indian princes and European capitalists, Mohammedans, Hindus, Parsees, Eurasians, Christians, pariahs—all must join in a convention and draft a constitution for an autonomous India within the empire and draw up the lines of such a home rule. This is the only way to avoid the breaking up of the empire.

I do not know how the Government of India and British bureaucracy look upon the "Manchester Guardian's" suggestion, and I hardly believe that Gandhi and his non-coöperators would agree to sit in a convention with European and Indian capitalists. But one thing is sure, and that is that no one questions, any more, India's right to home rule. It must come in one way or another. And nothing is more remarkable than the change of England's attitude to India since the beginning of the Gandhist movement. The European no longer scorns the Indian but treats him with consideration. Everybody agrees that it is a mistake to employ the violent methods which were the first the Governments resorted to in former days. From a spiritual and mental point of view, India is already victorious.

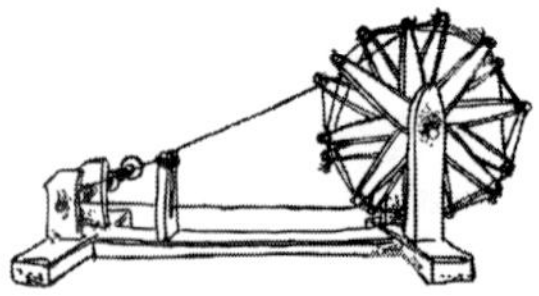

CHAPTER 5

And what will now come? Will England, wiser for past experiences, know how to mold the aspirations of the people of India? And will this people remain true to its ideal? Nations have short memories, and I should have but slight faith in India's power to remain true to the Mahatma's teaching if his doctrines were not an expression of the deepest and most ancient longings of the race. For if there is such a thing as genius, great by its own strength whether or not it corresponds to the ideals of its surroundings, there can be no genius of action, no leader, who does not incarnate the instincts of his race, satisfy the need of the hour, and requite the yearning of the world.

Mahatma Gandhi does all this. His principle of *Ahimsa* (non-violence) has been inscribed in the spirit of India for more than two thousand years. Mahavira, Buddha, and the cult of Vishnu have made it the substance of millions of souls. Gandhi has merely transfused heroic blood into it. He called upon the great shadows, the forces of the past, plunged in mortal lethargy, and at the sound of his voice they came to life. In him they found themselves. Gandhi is more than a word; he is an example. He incarnates the spirit of his people. Blessed the man who is a people, his people, entombed, and then resuscitated in him! But such resurrections are never haphazard. If the spirit of India now surges forth from temples and forests, it is because it holds the message for which the world is sighing.

This message carries far beyond the boundaries of India. India alone could formulate it, but it consecrates the nation's greatness as much as its sacrifice. It may become its cross.

For it would seem as if a people must he sacrificed in order to give new life to the world. The Jews were sacrificed to their Messiah, whom they had borne for centuries in their thoughts, and whom they did not recognize when He finally flowered on the blood-stained cross. More fortunate, India has recognized her Messiah, and joyously the people march to the sacrifice which is to set them free.

But, like the early Christians, they do not all understand the real meaning of their liberation. For a long time the Christians awaited the fulfilment of the *adveniat regnum tuum.* In India there are many who do not see beyond *Swaraj*, home rule. Incidentally, I imagine that this political goal will soon be reached. Europe, bled by wars and revolutions, impoverished and exhausted, despoiled of her prestige in the eyes of Asia, which she formerly oppressed, cannot long resist on Asiatic soil the aspirations of the awakened peoples of Islam, India, China, and Japan. But this would mean little, no matter how rich and new might be the harmonies which a few more nations would bring to the human symphony; this would mean little, if the surging spirit of Asia did not become the vehicle for a new ideal of life and of death, and, what is more, of action, for all humanity, and if it did not bring a new viaticum to prostrate Europe.

The world is swept by the wind of violence. This storm which ravages the harvest of our civilization did not break out from a clear sky. Centuries of brutal national pride, whetted by the idolatrous ideology of the Revolution, spread by the empty mockery of democracies, and crowned by a century of inhuman industrialism, rapacious plutocracy, and a materialistic system of economics where the soul perishes, stifled to death, were bound to culminate in these dark struggles where the treasures of the West succumbed. It is not enough to say all this was inevitable. There is a in it. Each people kills the other in the name of the same principles which hid the same covetousness and Cainish instincts. All—be they nationalists, Fascists, Bolshevists, members of the oppressed classes, members of the oppressing classes—claim that they have the right to use force, while refusing this right to others. Half a century ago might dominated right. To-day things are far worse. Might *is* right. Might has devoured right.

In the old crumbling world, no refuge, no hope, no great light. The church gives innocuous advice, virtuous and dosed, carefully worded so as not to antagonize the mighty. Besides, the church never sets the example—even when giving advice. Weak pacifists bray languishingly, and you feel that they hesitate and fumble, talk about a faith they no longer believe in. Who will prove this faith? And how, in an unbelieving world? Faith is proved by action.

This is the great message to the world, or, as Gandhi puts it, India's message—*self-sacrifice.*

And Tagore has repeated the same inspired words, for on this proud principle Tagore and Gandhi agree.

I hope this spirit of sacrifice will grow, and also the will to suffer... This is real liberty. Nothing is higher, not even national independence. The West has an unshakable belief in force and material wealth; therefore no matter how much it cries for peace and disarmament, its ferocity will cry still louder... We, in India, must show the world what this truth is which not only makes disarmament possible but transmutes it into strength. The fact that moral force is a stronger power than brute force will be proved by an unarmed people. The evolution of life shows that it has gradually cast off its formidable armature of scales and carapaces and a monstrous quantity of flesh until man was evolved who conquered brute force. The day will come when a weak, noble man absolutely unarmed will prove that the meek shall inherit the earth. It is logical that Mahatma Gandhi, weak of body and without material resources, should prove the unconquerable strength of the meek and the humble hidden in the heart of the outraged and destitute humanity of India. India's destiny is bound up in *Narayana* and not in *Narayani-sena*, in soul force and not muscle. It must uplift human history, transport it from the confused valley of material struggles to the high plateaux of spiritual battles. Although we may delude ourselves through phrases acquired from the vocabulary of the West, *Swaraj*, home rule, is not really our goal. Our battle is a spiritual battle, a fight for humanity. We must emancipate man from the meshes he has woven around him, free him from the organizations of national selfishness. We must persuade the butterfly that the freedom of

> the sky is better than the shelter of the cocoon. In India we have no word for "nation." When we loan the word from other peoples it is not suited to us, for we should ally ourselves with *Narayana*, the Supreme Being, and our victory will be the victory for God's world... If we can defy the powerful, the rich, the armed, by showing the world the power of the immortal spirit, the castle of the giant Flesh will crumble into nothingness. And then man will find real *Swaraj*. We, the miserable outcasts of the Orient, we must conquer freedom for all humanity...

"Our object," Gandhi has said, "is friendship with the whole world. Non-violence has come to men, and it will remain. It is the annunciation of peace on earth."

The peace of the world is far off. We have no illusions. We have seen, abundantly, during the course of half a century, the hypocrisy, the cowardice, and the cruelty of mankind. But this does not prevent us from loving mankind. For even among the worst there is a *nescio quid Dei*. We know the material ties that weigh on twentieth-century Europe, the crushing determinism of economic conditions which hem it in; we know that centuries of passions and systematized error have built a crust about our souls which the light cannot pierce. But we also know what miracles the spirit can work.

Historians, we have seen its glory brighten skies even darker than our own. We, who live but a day, have caught in India the sound of the tambour of Çiva, "*the Master Dancer who veils his devouring eye and guards his steps to save the world from plunging into the abyss.*"[1]

The *Realpolitiker* of violence, whether revolutionary or reactionary, ridicule our faith, and reveal thereby their ignorance of deep reality. Let them jeer! I have this faith. I know it is scorned and persecuted in Europe, and that in my own land we are but a handful—are we even a handful?—who believe in it. And even if I were the only one to believe in it, what would it matter? The true characteristic of faith is not to deny the hostility of the world, but to recognize it and to believe in spite of it! Faith is a battle. And our non-violence is the most desperate battle. The way to peace is not through weakness. We do not fight violence so much as weakness. Nothing is worthwhile unless it is strong, neither good nor evil. Absolute evil is better than emasculated goodness. Moaning pacifism is the death-knell of peace; it is cowardice and lack of faith. Let those who do not believe, who fear, withdraw! The way to peace leads through self-sacrifice.

This is Gandhi's message. The only thing lacking is the cross.[2] Every one knows that had it not been for the Jews, Rome would not have given it to Christ. The British Empire is no better than ancient Rome. The impetus has been given. The soul of Oriental peoples has been moved in its deepest fibers, and its vibrations are felt the whole world over.

The great religious apparitions of the Orient are ruled by a rhythm. One thing is certain: either Gandhi's spirit will triumph, or it will manifest itself again, as were manifested, centuries before, the Messiah and Buddha, till there finally is manifested,

1. Fragment of the oldest Invocation of Çiva, in the play "Mudra-Rakshasha" (400) by Vishakadatta.
2. This is the standpoint of the "conscientious objectors" in England, which is spreading little by little to other countries.

in a mortal half-god, the perfect incarnation of the principle of life which will lead a new humanity on to a new path.

OTHER HARDBACK BOOKS

- 1984 by George Orwell
  Fiction/Classics, ISBN: 9788193545836
- Abraham Lincoln by Lord Charnwood
  Biographies/Leaders, ISBN: 9789387669147
- Alice's Adventures in Wonderland by Lewis Carroll
  Children's/Classics, ISBN: 9789387669055
- Animal Farm by George Orwell
  Fiction/Classics, ISBN: 9789387669062
- Anthem by Ayn Rand
  Fiction/Classics, ISBN: 9789389157178
- As a Man Thinketh by James Allen
  Fiction/Classics, ISBN: 9789388118422
- Awakened Imagination by Neville Goddard
  Religion & Spirituality, ISBN: 9789389157185
- Be What You Wish by Neville Goddard
  Mind, Body & Spirit, ISBN: 9789388118163
- Becoming a Writer by Dorothea Brande
  Self Help/General, ISBN: 9789389157192
- Believe in Yourself by Joseph Murphy
  Mind, Body & Spirit, ISBN: 9789388118439
- Black Beauty by Anna Sewell
  Children's/Classics, ISBN: 9789388118262
- Civilization and Its Discontents by Sigmund Freud
  Social Sciences/General, ISBN: 9789388118279
- Demian by Hermann Hesse
  Fiction/Classics, ISBN: 9789388118170
- Feeling is the Secret by Neville Goddard
  Religion & Spirituality, ISBN: 9789389157208

Search the book by its ISBN

OTHER HARDBACK BOOKS

- Gitanjali by Rabindranath Tagore
  Fiction/Poems, ISBN: 9789387669079
- Great Speeches of Abraham Lincoln by Abraham Lincoln
  History/United States, ISBN: 9789387669154
- How to Attract Money by Joseph Murphy
  Self Help/Success, ISBN: 9789388118446
- How to be Filled with the Holy Spirit by A.W. Tozer
  Religion/Christianity, ISBN: 9789389157215
- How to Enjoy Your Life and Your Job by Dale Carnegie
  Self Help/General, ISBN: 9789388118293
- Illust. Biography of William Shakespeare by Manju Gupta
  Biographies/Authors, ISBN: 9789387669246
- Madhubala by Manju Gupta
  Biographies/Cinems, ISBN: 9789387669253
- Mansarover 1 (Hindi) by Premchand
  Fiction/Short Stories, ISBN: 9789387669086
- Meditations by Marcus Aurelius
  Non Fiction/Philosopy, ISBN: 9789388118781
- My Inventions: The Autobio. of Nikola Tesla by Nikola Tesla
  Autobiographies/Scientists, ISBN: 9789388118187
- Selected Stories of Rabindranath Tagore by Rabindranath Tagore
  Fiction/Short Stories, ISBN: 9789387669307
- Sense and Sensibility by Jane Austen
  Fiction/Classics, ISBN: 9789387669109
- Siddhartha by Hermann Hesse
  Fiction/Classics, ISBN: 9789387669116
- Tales from India by Rudyard Kipling
  Fiction/Short Stories, ISBN: 9789387669123

Search the book by its ISBN

OTHER HARDBACK BOOKS

- Tales from Shakespeare by Charles Lamb, Mary Lamb
  Fiction/Short Stories, ISBN: 9789387669314
- The Alchemy of Happiness by Al-Ghazzali
  Religion & Spirituality, ISBN: 9789388118309
- The Art of Public Speaking by Dale Carnegie
  Self Help/General, ISBN: 9789388118477
- The Autobiography of a Yogi by Paramahansa Yogananda
  Autobiographies/General, ISBN: 9789387669192
- The Dynamic Laws of Prosperity by Catherine Ponder
  Mind, Body & Spirit, ISBN: 9789388118194
- The Elements of Style by William Strunk
  Non Fiction/Skill, ISBN: 9789389157222
- The Game of Life and How to Play It by Florence Scovel Shinn
  Mind, Body & Spirit, ISBN: 9789388118316
- The Imitation of Christ by Thomas À Kempis
  Religion/Christianity, ISBN: 9789388118200
- The Jungle Book by Rudyard Kipling
  Children's/Classics, ISBN: 9789387669338
- The Knowledge of the Holy by A.W. Tozer
  Religion/Christianity, ISBN: 9789389157239
- The Light of Asia by Sir Edwin Arnold
  Fiction/Poetry, ISBN: 9789387669130
- The Magic of Faith by Joseph Murphy
  Mind, Body & Spirit, ISBN: 9789388118712
- The Origin of Species by Charles Darwin
  Sciences/Life Sciences, ISBN: 9789387669345
- The Path of Prosperity by James Allen
  Mind, Body & Spirit, ISBN: 9789388118323

Search the book by its ISBN

OTHER HARDBACK BOOKS

- The Power of Awareness by Neville Goddard
  Mind, Body & Spirit, ISBN: 9789388118330
- The Power of Concentration by Theron Q. Dumont
  Self Help/General, ISBN: 9789388118224
- The Power of Positive Thinking by Norman Vincent Peale
  Mind, Body & Spirit, ISBN: 9789388118729
- The Prophet by Kahlil Gibran
  Fiction/Classics, ISBN: 9789388118453
- The Psychopathology of Everyday Life by Sigmund Freud
  Non Fiction/Psychology, ISBN: 9789388118231
- The Pursuit of God by A.W. Tozer
  Religion/Christianity, ISBN: 9789389157246
- The Quick and Easy Way to Effec. Speaking by Dale Carnegie
  Self Help/General, ISBN: 9789388118347
- The Science of Getting Rich by Wallace D. Wattles
  Self Help/Success, ISBN: 9789387669239
- The Seven Laws of Teaching by John Milton Gregory
  Self Help/General, ISBN: 9789388118460
- The Upanishads by Swami Paramananda
  Religion/Hinduism, ISBN: 9789388118774
- The World as I See It by Albert Einstein
  Non Fiction/Philosopy, ISBN: 9789388118248
- Thought Vibration by William Walker Atkinson
  Non Fiction/Philosopy, ISBN: 9789389157253
- Wake Up and Live! by Dorothea Brande
  Mind, Body & Spirit, ISBN: 9789388118255
- Your Faith is Your Fortune by Neville Goddard
  Religion & Spirituality, ISBN: 9789389157260

Search the book by its ISBN